GUITAR SOLOING BASICS

Techniques, Scales, Theory, and Lots of Licks
for Playing Lead Guitar in a Variety of Styles

BY JEFF CLEMENTI

PLAYBACK+
Speed • Pitch • Balance • Loop

To access audio visit:
www.halleonard.com/mylibrary
Enter Code
4961-6341-8430-3812

ISBN 978-1-4950-8060-9

HAL•LEONARD®
7777 W. BLUEMOUND RD. P.O. BOX 13819 MILWAUKEE, WI 53213

T0056093

Copyright © 2017 by HAL LEONARD LLC
International Copyright Secured   All Rights Reserved

No part of this publication may be reproduced in any form or by any means
without the prior written permission of the Publisher.

In Australia Contact:
Hal Leonard Australia Pty. Ltd.
4 Lentara Court
Cheltenham, Victoria, 3192 Australia
Email: ausadmin@halleonard.com.au

Visit Hal Leonard Online at
www.halleonard.com

CONTENTS

PAGE

4   Introduction to Soloing

4   The Three Components of Soloing

5   Methods of Soloing

5   Keys

5   About the Book

6   Reading Scale Diagrams

6   Moving a Scale

7   Reading Tablature

7   Getting Started

9   PART I

10   The Minor Pentatonic Scale

11   Repeating Patterns

12   Sample Solo 1

13   The Whole-Step Bend

14   The Bend and Release

15   The Hammer-On and Pull-Off

16   Two More Whole-Step Bends

17   Sample Solo 2

18   The Bend and Release with a Pull-Off

19   Exercises Using the Hammer-On and Pull-Off

20   The Slight Bend

21   Vibrato

22   Exercise Using the Slight Bend

22   Exercise Using Vibrato

22   More Three-Note Repeating Patterns

23   Unmeasured Slides

24   Sample Solo 3

24   Altering a Lick

27   Sample Solo 4

28   The Blues Scale

29   The Half-Step Bend

30   The Unison Bend

31   Double Stops

32   Measured Slides

33   Sample Solo 5

34   The Extended Minor Pentatonic Scale

35   First Finger Whole-Step Bends

36   Connecting Scales

37   Exercises Using the Extended Minor Pentatonic Scale

38   The Pre-Bend

39   More Bends with One Note

40   The Double-Stop Bend

41   Sample Solo 6

42   The Extended Blues Scale

43   The Major Pentatonic Scales

44   The Extended Major Pentatonic Scales

44   More About Form-Equivalent Scales
45   Licks and Form-Equivalent Scales
45   Effective Soloing
46   Sample Solo 7
48   Sample Solo 8
49   The Hybrid Major Pentatonic Scale
50   Sample Solo 9

51   *PART II*
52   The Modes
54   The Aeolian Mode
55   Sample Solo 10
56   The Dorian Mode
57   Sample Solo 11
58   The Phrygian Mode
59   Sample Solo 12
60   The Ionian Mode
61   Sample Solo 13
62   The Mixolydian Mode
63   Sample Solo 14
63   The Lydian Mode
65   Sample Solo 15
65   The Phrygian Dominant Scale
67   Sample Solo 16

68   *PART III*
68   The Five Scale Forms
69   Memorizing the Five Scale Forms

81   *PART IV*
81   Introduction to Chordal Soloing
82   Pentatonic Scales with Chords
82   Sample Solo 17
83   Sample Solo 18
84   Phrygian Dominant Scale with Chords
84   Sample Solo 19
85   Sample Solo 20
86   Minor Pentatonic Scale with Major 3rds
87   Sample Solo 21
88   Sixths
89   Sample Solo 22
90   Finger Tapping
91   Sample Solo 23

92   Appendix – The Backing Tracks
96   About the Author

INTRODUCTION TO SOLOING

So you want to create your own exciting guitar solos? When you see an accomplished guitarist soloing, it probably looks pretty easy, as if there were no rules or guidelines to follow, as if the solo was coming from pure inspiration. But looks can be deceiving.

As you work through this book, you will find there is much to learn and master in order to play that seamless, effortless guitar solo. Some of what you learn will be easy, but some of it may be difficult, too. However, through diligent practice, you should be able to overcome any initial obstacles and be on your way to becoming a skilled soloist on the guitar.

The guitar soloing described in this book, which is used by the majority of players in the popular music field, is actually a blues-based style. Throughout the course of several decades, guitarists such as Chuck Berry, Eric Clapton, Eddie Van Halen, and Kirk Hammett have all produced music that sounds quite different from one another, yet they all share a common foundation based upon the elements found in blues guitar playing.

This book will reveal those blues-based elements and more. After mastering its contents, you will have gained the knowledge and tools to touch and talk to people through your soloing. And who knows? One day you may find yourself in front of thousands of adoring fans, creating guitar solos like the aforementioned guitarists!

So let's get started! And be sure to study and practice hard because the more effort you put in, the more you'll be rewarded!

THE THREE COMPONENTS OF SOLOING

The three components listed below are essential ingredients to soloing. Study their definitions and different uses.

1. **SCALES:** A scale is a group of notes played in succession. Each scale has a letter name—ranging from A to G—that is derived from one note in the scale, the *tonic*. There are many kinds of scales; all can be described as different sounds or colors to be used at the discretion of the soloist. The soloist will mix the notes of a scale in various ways to create melodic ideas, or *licks*.

2. **TECHNIQUES:** A *technique* is the physical left-hand finger maneuvers used to embellish the notes, such as bending, sliding, or the like. Integrating the various techniques into one's playing allows the guitarist to be more expressive, which results in a solo that is more exciting and has more life and feeling.

3. **LICKS:** A *lick* is one or more notes taken from a scale and played in different rhythms and with one or more techniques. You can think of a solo as being many licks strung together to form a coherent melody. Licks are usually created spontaneously as the solo progresses, but occasionally memorized licks may also be added. Memorizing other guitarists' licks is beneficial because you can always fall back on those licks if you temporarily run out of ideas while soloing. Learning other guitarists' licks will also give you the opportunity to see how they were created with the various scales and techniques, which may give you more insight when creating your own licks. Experienced soloists usually alter their memorized licks to fit the solo more perfectly and to inject their own personality into them.

METHODS OF SOLOING

There are two methods used for soloing: *modal* and *chordal*. Modal soloing is the favored method of blues-based guitar players and also the method that you will use for most of this book. Chordal soloing is more often employed by jazz guitarists and is introduced in the latter pages. Below are the definitions of these two methods of soloing:

Modal Soloing: soloing with one scale over a chord progression without necessarily having or needing any knowledge of the chords being played.

Chordal Soloing: soloing with different scales that match and change according to the individual chords being played over. This method requires knowing the names, quality, and function of the chords being played.

KEYS

Every piece of popular music is in a *key*. A key can be defined simply as an organization of notes with a central note and chord from which the music leaves and returns. A more thorough definition is not important for the purpose of this book, but there are a couple of features about keys and their relationship to soloing that you should know.

First, each key has a letter name, ranging from A to G (like scales). Secondly, there are two qualities of keys: *major* and *minor*. Modal soloing requires you to be in the same key as the music, which means the tonic of the scale being used must match the letter name of the key. You will also need to consider the major or minor quality of a key when determining which scales to use. These items will be examined more closely as you work through the book.

ABOUT THE BOOK

This book is organized into four sections. Part I is the largest section and contains all of the popular scales and techniques that guitarists use for soloing. Part II covers some other colorful scales: the modes. Part III contains additional forms of the scales that were studied in the first two sections. After using the modal method of soloing for the first three sections of the book, chordal soloing is finally introduced in Part IV.

This book also includes hundreds of licks that will incorporate any new material you learn. Once in a while, exercises will be introduced to help you gain more dexterity with a particular scale or technique. Of course, there is ample instruction explaining how to use everything presented.

Lastly, the first page of this book contains an internet address that you can use to access the audio tracks that demonstrate the various licks, techniques, and sample solos in the book. Everything recorded in the audio portion is indicated in the book by a track number (e.g., Track 67). Besides these demonstration tracks, there are 17 additional backing tracks consisting of a recorded rhythm section made up of drums, bass, and keyboards—12 tracks to practice modal soloing and the remaining five to practice chordal soloing.

READING SCALE DIAGRAMS

Letter name of scale
(same as tonic)

Name of scale

G Minor Pentatonic Scale

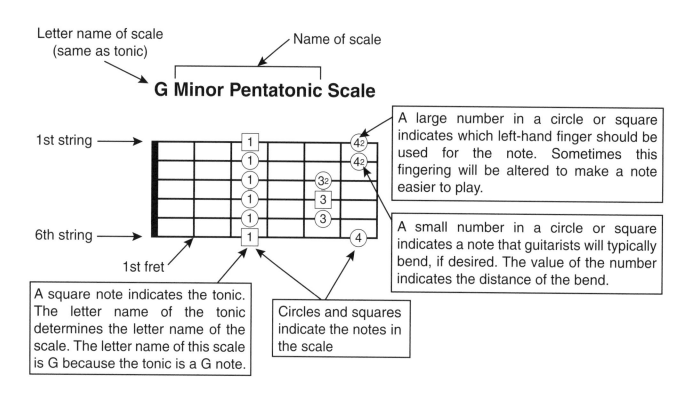

1st string

6th string

1st fret

A large number in a circle or square indicates which left-hand finger should be used for the note. Sometimes this fingering will be altered to make a note easier to play.

A small number in a circle or square indicates a note that guitarists will typically bend, if desired. The value of the number indicates the distance of the bend.

A square note indicates the tonic. The letter name of the tonic determines the letter name of the scale. The letter name of this scale is G because the tonic is a G note.

Circles and squares indicate the notes in the scale

SMALL NUMBERS KEY

As noted above, the value of a small number in a circle indicates the distance of a bend. The numbers are measured in increments of a half step, which equals one fret. Thus, if there is a small number "2" in a circle, it means that the note should be bent two half steps, which equals a whole step. If there are two small numbers in a circle, then the note can be bent to either distance indicated by the numbers. See below:

1 (half step) = Half-Step Bend

2 (half steps) = Whole-Step Bend

3 (half steps) = 1 1/2-Step Bend

The actual execution of each bend will be explained as you work through the book.

MOVING A SCALE

When moving a scale, first locate one of its tonic notes in the formation. Using the fingerboard diagram below, move the scale so that this note is on the fret with the desired letter name. For example, if you want to play in the key of A, the aforementioned G minor pentatonic scale should be moved up two frets, where the tonic will be on an A note.

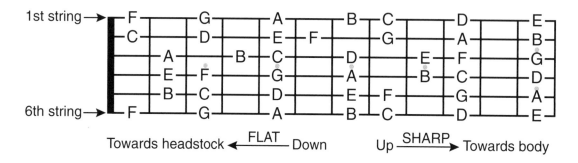

1st string

6th string

Towards headstock ← FLAT — Down   Up — SHARP → Towards body

More About the Fingerboard Diagram: The unlabeled frets are notes that also have names. Look at the symbols below. These symbols, called *accidentals*, are used to alter the "natural" notes and move them to these unlabeled frets.

- A sharp (♯) raises a note one fret (towards the body of the guitar).

- A flat (♭) lowers a note one fret (towards the headstock).

For example, an F♯ tonic on the sixth string would be located on the second fret, an E♭ tonic on the fifth string would be located on the sixth fret, and a C♭ tonic (the same as a B note) on the fourth string would be located on the ninth fret. (Notes can have more than one name, but try not to let their alternate names confuse you.)

READING TABLATURE

Tablature, or "tab," is a system used for reading notes on the guitar and will be used throughout this book. The example below illustrates how to read it.

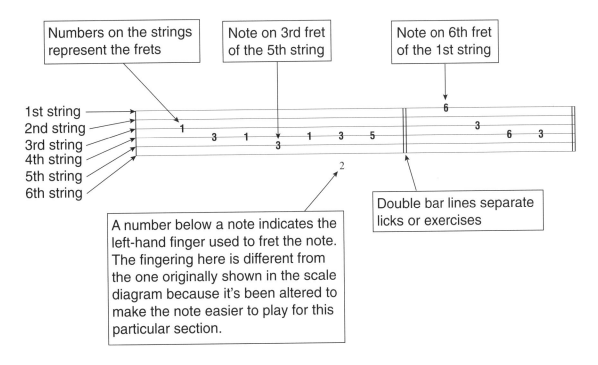

Numbers on the strings represent the frets

Note on 3rd fret of the 5th string

Note on 6th fret of the 1st string

A number below a note indicates the left-hand finger used to fret the note. The fingering here is different from the one originally shown in the scale diagram because it's been altered to make the note easier to play for this particular section.

Double bar lines separate licks or exercises

GETTING STARTED

USING THE THREE COMPONENTS

1. **SCALES:** Practice playing each scale from the scale diagrams in the book. When going up a scale, begin with the sixth string and play the notes from left to right; when going down a scale, begin with the first string and play the notes from right to left. Then try playing the scale along with the audio track. The scale is played from its lowest to highest note and then back again. Once you are comfortable playing the scale, move it up the fingerboard to different locations and identify its letter name according to the tonic.

2. **TECHNIQUES:** Read the directions in the book explaining how to properly execute a technique and then listen to the audio track to hear how it should sound. Try to copy the techniques as accurately as possible. Be particularly careful when copying any pitch variations that may be part of the technique, such as with string bending. Practice each technique so that your execution is flawless and

effortless—a smooth, expressive solo can't be created if you are struggling with your guitar. Here's a tip: many of the techniques will be much easier to execute if you use lighter gauge strings on your electric guitar. An .008, .009, or .010 gauge string set is highly recommended.

3. **LICKS:** Licks are introduced every time a new scale or technique is presented and are of four-beat and eight-beat durations. (Some four-beat licks are two-beat licks played twice. Eventually, you will be rhythmically altering the licks, which may change their location in a measure or the number of licks that will fit into a measure.) To play a lick, first study the rhythms of the notes and the techniques being used in it. Examine where the notes are located in the scale from which the lick was created. Then listen to the lick as it's played on the audio track and try to reproduce it as perfectly as possible. After learning a lick, try memorizing it so you can incorporate it into your future solos.

USING THE BACKING TRACKS

A listing of the 17 backing tracks is located in the Appendix. Backing Tracks 1–12 will be used for modal soloing (Parts I and II) and Backing Tracks 13–17 will be used later for chordal soloing (Part IV). Each listing for Backing Tracks 1–12 indicates the key of the track and the appropriate scales that can be used for soloing over that particular track. The chord progressions used for each track are also included and can be played by another guitarist while you practice soloing or vice versa. Follow the three steps below while using Backing Tracks 1–12 for modal soloing:

1. Choose a track that matches the scale you want to use. For example, if you want to play licks created from the Phrygian dominant scale, use Backing Track 11 or 12.

2. Move the scale on the fingerboard to match the key of the track. If you are already in the correct key, go to Step 3.

3. Play the backing track. While playing the track, use either of these two methods to create a solo: 1) build and connect your own licks by mixing up the notes of the scale, or 2) connect in different orders the various licks that were created from that particular scale.

When employing the first method, begin by using only the notes of the scale that are on the first string, playing these notes in a quarter-note rhythm, then adding an eighth-note rhythm. Eventually, add the second string, progressing to the remaining four strings as you feel more confident. Then experiment with other rhythms. As you progress through the book, incorporate any new techniques that you learn into your licks, too.

When employing the second method, first choose a lick and repeat it many times with the track. Then do the same with another lick, and then another. Eventually, try stringing different licks together to form a solo.

After you gain some experience using both methods, start combining them: create your own licks (as in the first method) and then occasionally interject any licks that you've learned and memorized. This may seem hard at first, but as your soloing matures, it should get easier, to the point where you're not thinking much about it at all.

PART I

In Part I, you will begin your studies of modal soloing by learning one of the most revered scales of blues-based guitarists: the *minor pentatonic scale*. It has been used to create innumerable classic solos in every musical style. Later, you will learn another favorite of guitarists: the *blues scale*. As you reach the end of Part I, you will be exposed to the happier-sounding *major pentatonic scale*. The extended forms of these scales will also be explored, as they are an important soloing tool because of their larger range of notes and wider horizontal spread across the fingerboard.

Besides an abundance of scales, Part I includes all of the popular techniques used by blues-based guitar players: hammer-ons, pull-offs, vibrato, various bends, slides, and more. These techniques, when properly executed, will make you sound like an accomplished and polished guitar soloist.

Part I is the most important and valuable section in this book. It possesses all of the tools and information that you need to become a formidable and exciting lead guitarist, so study it carefully!

THE MINOR PENTATONIC SCALE

Shown below is the G minor pentatonic scale. Practice playing it. Remember: moving a scale up or down the fingerboard will change its letter name, depending on where the tonic is located.

Notice that the scale has three notes that guitarists typically bend a whole step (notes with small numbers). The bending of these notes will be explained fully in the upcoming pages of this section; for now, however, just familiarize yourself with their location within the scale.

Once you are able to play the scale proficiently, practice the licks that follow.

TRACK 1

G Minor Pentatonic Scale

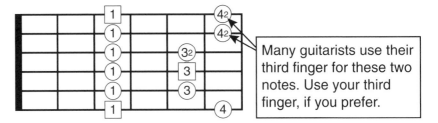

Many guitarists use their third finger for these two notes. Use your third finger, if you prefer.

Licks Created from the G Minor Pentatonic Scale:

TRACKS 2–9

REPEATING PATTERNS

You can make your solos more interesting by incorporating repeating patterns into them. A *repeating pattern* is simply a group of notes played two or more times over a certain period of time. A lick that is repeated can also be regarded as a repeating pattern. Repeating patterns are easy to create and will provide the solo with a sort of resting point because of their repetitious and unifying nature.

Shown below are three sets of random repeating patterns: two-note, four-note, and three-note patterns. The three-note patterns are interesting because they do not conform to a measure of 4/4 time. When the two-note and four-note patterns are repeated, they will fit neatly into one measure. However, when the three-note pattern is repeated, it takes three measures for the pattern to start again on the first beat. This type of repeating pattern is called a *polyrhythm*.

Play the patterns by repeating each one many times. They are comprised entirely of eighth notes (musicians often use repeating patterns comprised of different numbers of notes and time values, too). Once you can play these patterns proficiently, practice putting them into your solos—you do not have to complete a pattern when you decide to exit it.

Repeating Patterns Created from the G Minor Pentatonic Scale:

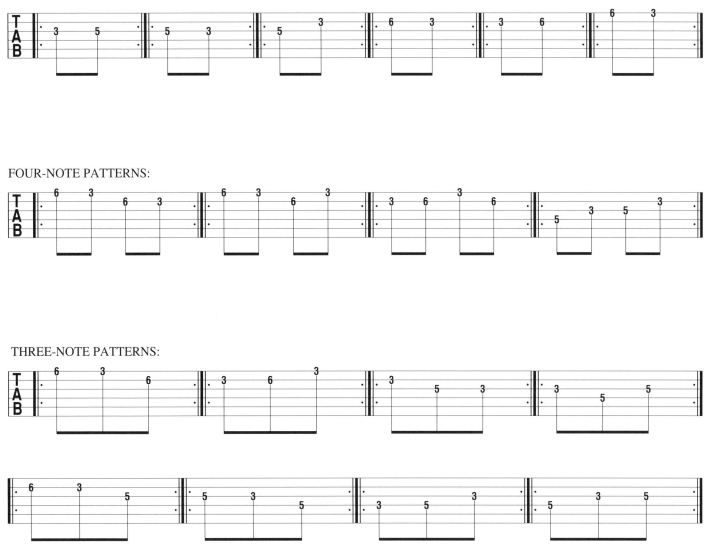

TWO-NOTE PATTERNS:

FOUR-NOTE PATTERNS:

THREE-NOTE PATTERNS:

SAMPLE SOLO 1

Shown below is a solo created from the material learned thus far. It is played over Backing Track 8. Listen to the solo on Track 10 and try to play along. Above the tab are brackets indicating the lick that is being used. After learning the solo, try creating your own solo over Backing Track 8, using the G minor pentatonic scale.

TRACK 10

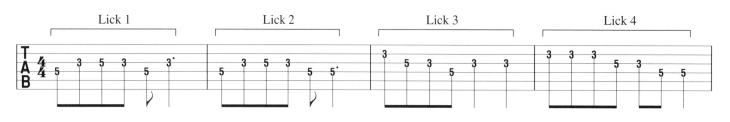

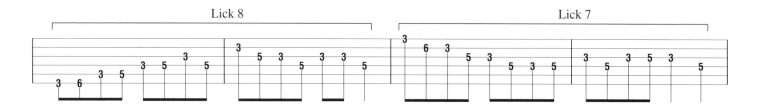

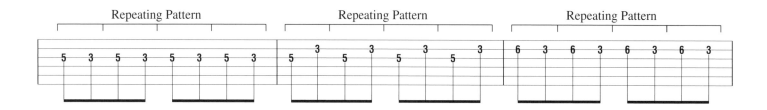

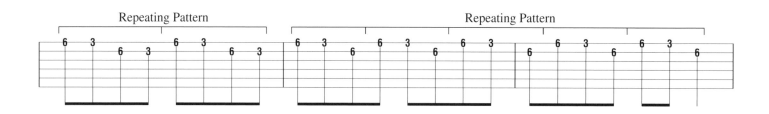

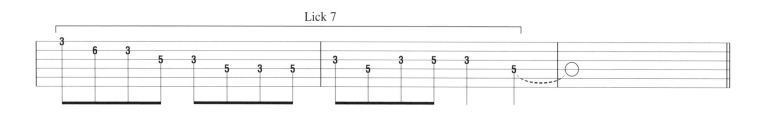

TECHNIQUE
THE WHOLE-STEP BEND

Bending a string to change the pitch of a note, executed by using one or more fingers to push the string upwards or pull it downwards, is commonplace for today's blues-based guitarist. As shown below, the bend is notated with a curved, upturned arrow and a numeral placed above the arrow to indicate the distance of the bend. Here, "1" indicates a *whole-step bend*. The subsequent note is not part of the technique; instead, it's used to check the pitch of the bent note.

To play the example, place your third finger on the fifth fret of the third string and your second finger below it, on the fourth fret. The added strength from using two fingers will make the string easier to bend. Now strike the string and bend it upward, towards the sixth string. Using your first finger, then play the second note without taking your other two fingers off the first (bent) note. While letting the strings ring simultaneously, try to match the pitch of the first note to the second note. Be careful not to bend the second-string note. Once you are able to play the example proficiently, try playing the bent note without the aid of the second note.

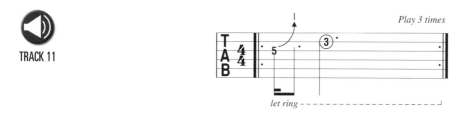

Now try playing the licks below, which incorporate this technique. Make sure that the sound of the bent note ends the moment the next note of the lick is played (unlike the previous example, where you let the bent note ring while playing the second note).

Whole-Step Bend Licks Created from the G Minor Pentatonic Scale:

TRACKS 12–20

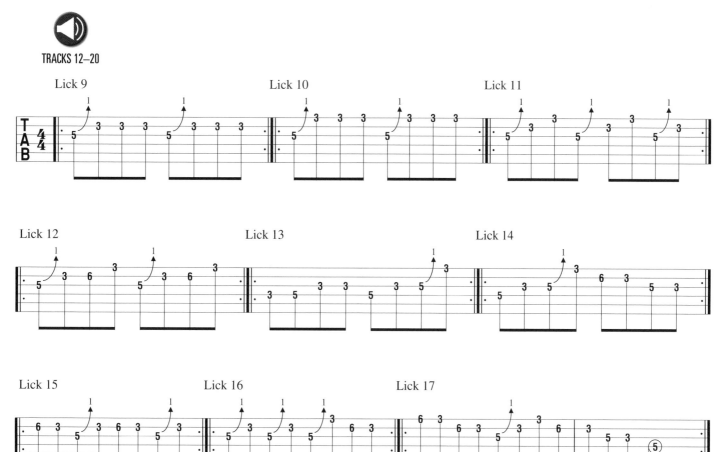

TECHNIQUE
THE BEND AND RELEASE

Shown below is a technique called the *bend and release*. The technique consists of striking a string, bending it the indicated distance, and then letting the string come back down to its original pitch, with no break in the sound. It's important to keep constant finger pressure on the string to prevent the sound from cutting out when being released.

This technique is notated with a curved, upturned arrow that is followed by one that turns downwards. Try playing the example.

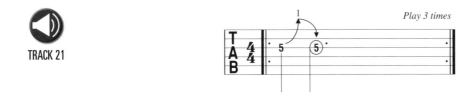

Once you are able to play the example proficiently, try playing the licks shown below.

Bend-and-Release Licks Created from the G Minor Pentatonic Scale:

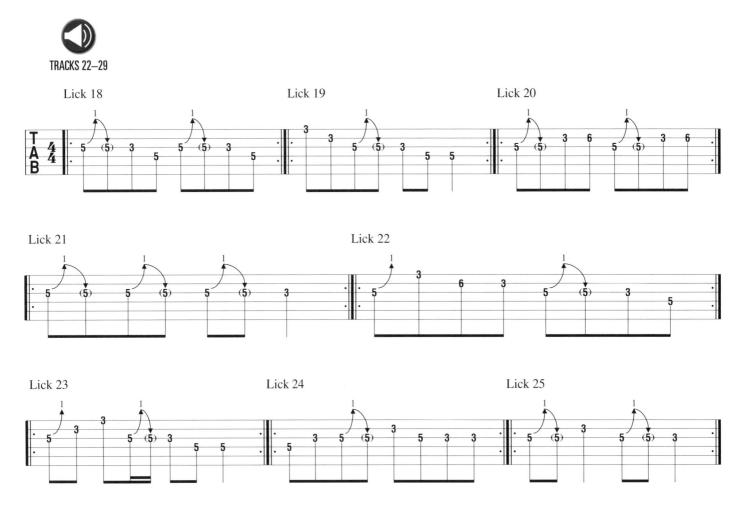

TRACKS 22–29

TECHNIQUE
THE HAMMER-ON AND PULL-OFF

The *hammer-on* and *pull-off* are techniques that involve two notes on the same string. With both techniques, the first note is struck and the second note is sounded by the physical maneuvering of one of the left-hand fingers. Notice that the second note is *not* struck in either technique.

The hammer-on and pull-off are indicated by a curved line (called a *slur*) placed over the notes. The difference between each technique is that the hammer-on starts with a lower note and ends on a higher note (see the first example), whereas the pull-off starts with a higher note and ends on a lower note (see the second example).

When playing the hammer-on in the first example, strike the first note and then use the third finger to hammer down on the second note to force it to sound. When playing the pull-off in the second example, strike the first note and then use the third finger to pull downward on the string so that the second note is forced to sound.

The third and fourth examples combine both techniques. When playing the third example, strike the first note, hammer onto the second note, and then pull off to the original (first) note. When playing the fourth example, strike the first note, pull off to the second note, and then hammer onto the original (first) note. Again, only the first note is struck in these examples.

TRACKS 30–33

Once you are able to play the examples proficiently, try playing the licks below.

Hammer-On and Pull-Off Licks Created from the G Minor Pentatonic Scale:

TRACKS 34–42

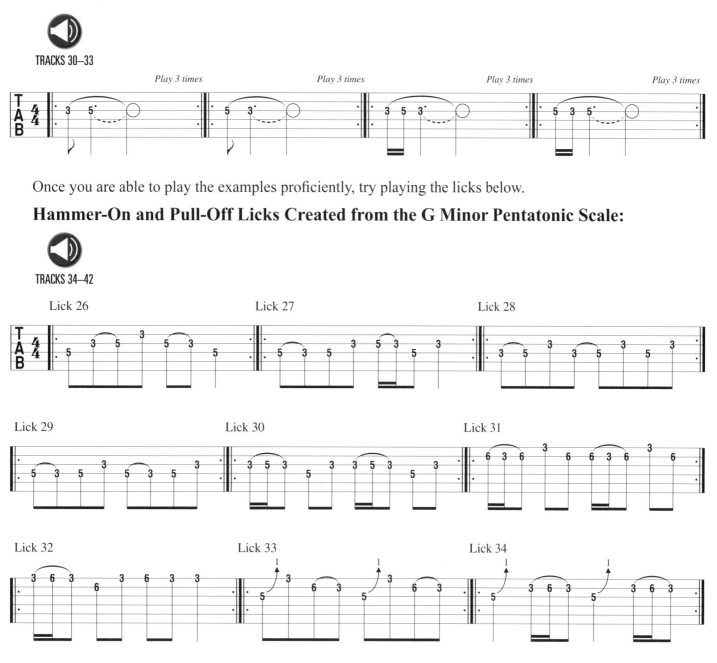

TECHNIQUE
TWO MORE WHOLE-STEP BENDS

Shown in the examples below are the other two notes in the minor pentatonic scale that are typically bent a whole step. When playing either example, use the fourth finger, with the third finger helping to push the string upwards, as you similarly did with the third and second finger for the third-string whole-step bend.

In the first example, the whole-step bend is on the second string. Try playing it, making sure that the pitch of the first (bent) note matches the second note. In the second example, because the bend is executed on the first string, there are no other strings with which to match it, but you can test its pitch correctness by comparing it with the note on the eighth fret of the first string. Try playing it.

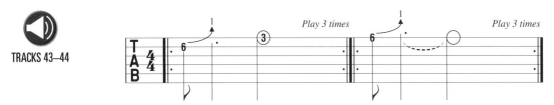

TRACKS 43–44

Once you are proficient at playing the two examples, try playing the licks shown below. As with the first whole-step bend you learned, make sure that the sound of the bent note ends the moment the next note is played. But first, here's a refresher on the notes typically bent in the minor pentatonic scale:

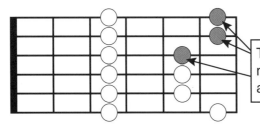

The gray notes shown here are the three notes in the minor pentatonic scale that are typically bent a whole step.

More Whole-Step Bend Licks Created from the G Minor Pentatonic Scale:

TRACKS 45–52

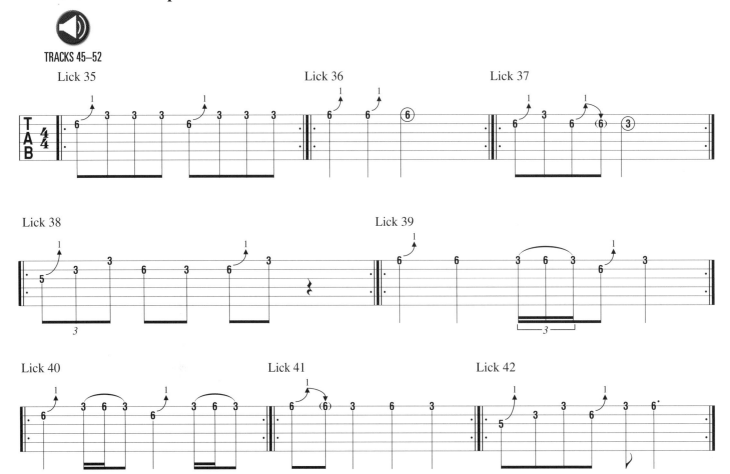

SAMPLE SOLO 2

Shown below is a solo created from the licks that you've learned so far. It is played over Backing Track 2 and is a popular song form called a 12-bar blues, the name partially derived from its 12-measure construction. Listen to Track 53 and try to play along. Also try creating your own solo over the backing track, using the G minor pentatonic scale.

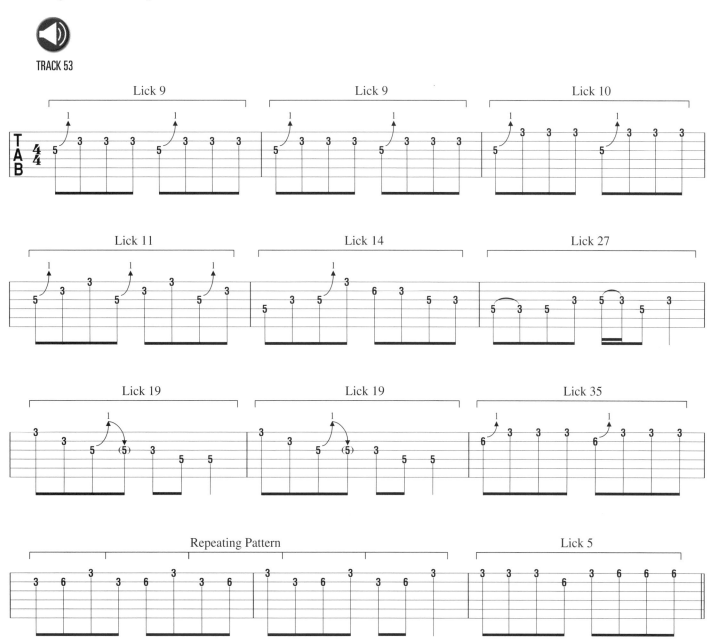

TRACK 53

After learning the solo, play it over Backing Tracks 1 and 8. You'll be surprised how different the solo sounds. Also try playing the solo with some of the other backing tracks—just make sure that you're in the correct key and that the minor pentatonic scale will work with whatever backing track you want to use. Refer to Backing Tracks 1–12 in the Appendix to check the key of each backing track and whether the minor pentatonic scale will work for the particular track you want to solo over.

TECHNIQUE
THE BEND AND RELEASE WITH A PULL-OFF

The *bend and release with a pull-off* is a very powerful technique that has been used by virtually every prominent guitarist. It is difficult to learn, but mastering it is well worth the effort because it can add so much emotion and excitement to a lick. This technique is indicated by the bend and release arrows, plus the addition of a curved line to show the pull-off.

Try playing the technique, as shown below. Make sure to execute the bend and release *before* doing the pull-off because the reverse action will usually not produce desirable results. Also, make sure that there is no break in the sound at any point. Finally, as a general rule, the first note (i.e., the bend) may be held indefinitely, but the release and pull-off is usually done very rapidly.

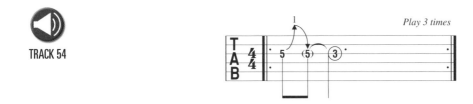

TRACK 54

Once you are able to play the example proficiently, try playing the licks below.

G Minor Pentatonic Licks Using the Bend and Release with a Pull-off:

TRACKS 55–63

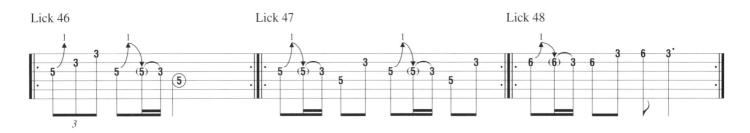

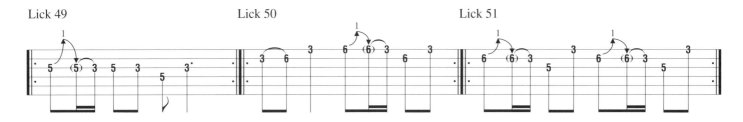

EXERCISES USING THE HAMMER-ON AND PULL-OFF

Exercises are important for two reasons:

1. Exercises build technique. This means that, by practicing them, you will be able to play faster and with greater dexterity and stamina. When soloing, it is important to be able to express on your guitar the musical ideas that pop into your head, so developing good technique will help overcome any physical limitations that might otherwise be encountered when trying to play those ideas.

2. Exercises also provide you with material that is suitable for your solos. If you get momentarily stuck without an idea, you can resort to the ideas contained in an exercise that you have practiced and memorized. Or, if your solos seem like they are sounding too much alike, analyzing the ideas from an exercise can help you break out of any redundancies.

Practice the four exercises below until you have them memorized and can play them with ease. Always start an exercise at a slow enough tempo so that you can play it correctly and in time. Then gradually increase the speed to the point where the exercise can be still be played without any sloppiness or mistakes. Each pattern is repeated ever two beats (i.e., played twice per measure).

Once you are able to play the exercises comfortably at a moderate tempo, try incorporating them into your solos—not necessarily an entire exercise, but just bits and pieces of it. But try to make those bits and pieces sound like they are an integral part of the solo—as if you had created them yourself!

Exercises Created from the G Minor Pentatonic Scale:

TRACKS 64–67

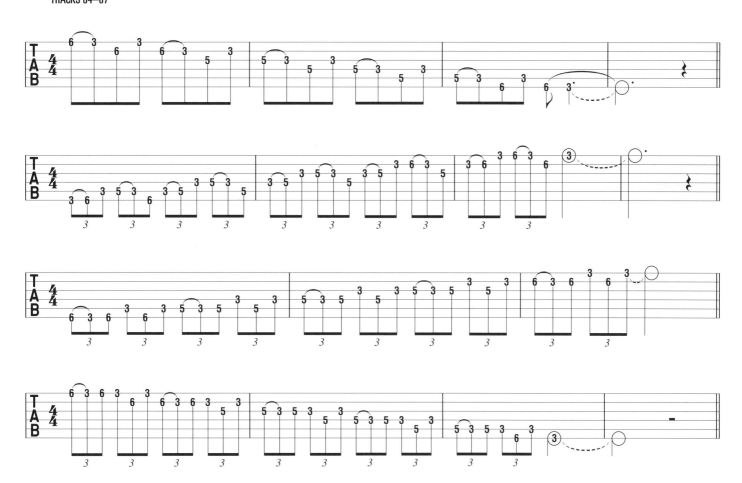

TECHNIQUE
THE SLIGHT BEND

A bend of a quarter step is called a *slight bend* and is indicated by the quarter-step designation (1/4) above the bend arrow. Unlike the three whole-step bends that you learned, the slight bend can be applied to any note in the scale.

The decision of whether to push the string upwards or pull it downwards is determined by the string that the slight bend is executed on: the first string must always be pushed upwards, whereas the sixth string must always be pulled downwards (if you bend these strings in the opposite directions, the strings will slide off the fingerboard). It doesn't matter which direction the four middle strings are bent, so use your own preference for these strings.

Since the slight bend can be applied to any note in the scale, it will sometimes be executed with the first finger, but this should not be difficult since the bend is so small. When executing the slight bend with any of the other fingers, use two fingers to help with the bending, if needed.

Try playing the example below. Make sure that the note does not reach the pitch of the next fret because it is easy to bend the string too far.

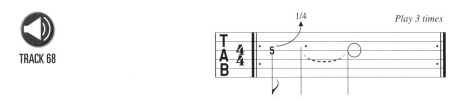

Once you are able to play the example proficiently, try playing the licks below.

Slight-Bend Licks Created from the G Minor Pentatonic Scale:

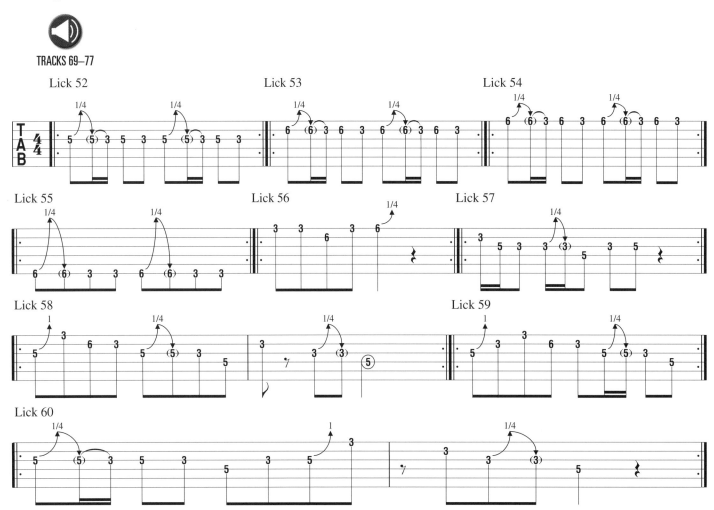

TECHNIQUE
VIBRATO

Vibrato is a technique that is usually used whenever a guitarist sustains a note for any length of time. It can be defined as a steady up-and-down wavering of pitch that gives a note more life and feeling. It is executed by striking the note once and then slightly bending and releasing the string many times in a row.

The range of a vibrato's wavering pitch can extend from small to wide. A small vibrato range would be a quarter step (slight bend); a wide-range vibrato would be a whole step or more, with the wideness depending on the strength of the guitarist's fingers. Even wider ranges of vibrato are possible with a whammy bar, although this device actually produces a wavering sound that results in a note that is *lowered* and then returned to its original pitch, whereas the fingered vibrato produces a wavering sound that results in a note that is *raised* and then returned to its original pitch.

The most useful and common vibrato is one with the smaller (quarter-step) range. Vibrato is indicated by a wavy line placed over the note, as shown below. The speed of the wavering of pitch is up to the performer; however, a medium-to-fast vibrato that is in time to the music is more common. Try playing the example.

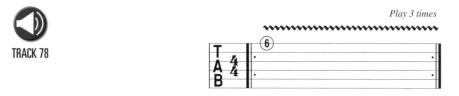

Once you are able to play the example proficiently, try playing the licks below.

Vibrato Licks Created from the G Minor Pentatonic Scale:

TRACKS 79–87

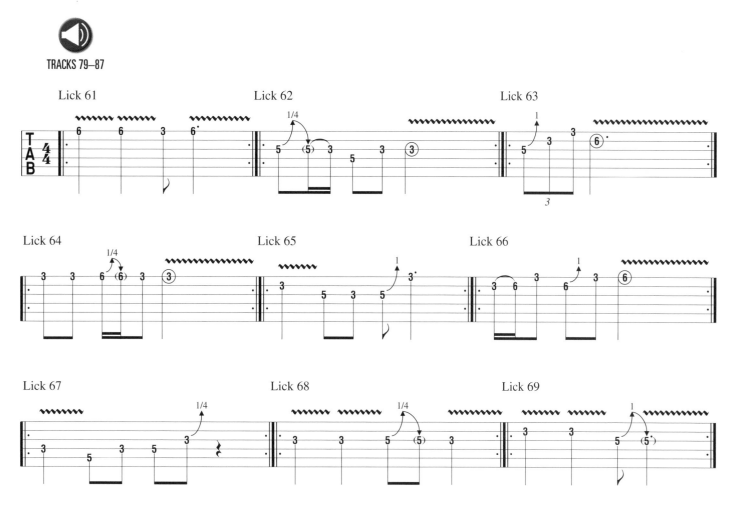

EXERCISE USING THE SLIGHT BEND

Play the notes evenly. Also try playing the exercise at different tempos.

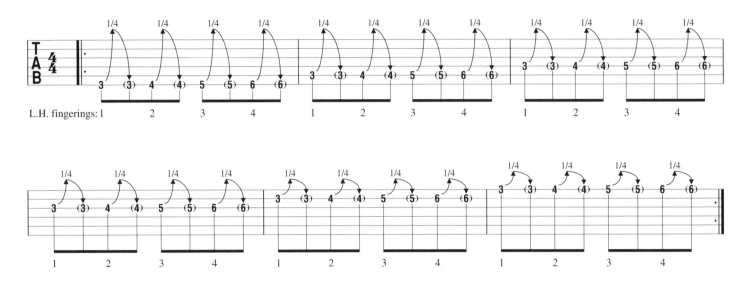

EXERCISE USING VIBRATO

Play the notes evenly. Also try playing the exercise at different tempos.

MORE THREE-NOTE REPEATING PATTERNS

Here are some more three-note repeating patterns, this time incorporating the whole-step bends that you learned.

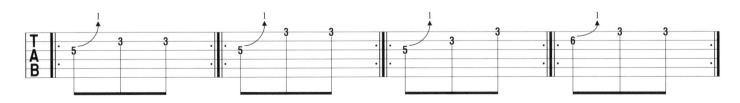

TECHNIQUE
UNMEASURED SLIDES

The *unmeasured slide* is a slide that has no specific starting, middle, or ending point, or any combination of these. It is usually executed quickly and occurs frequently at the beginning or end of a lick.

In the first example below, the note starts on an unspecified lower fret and then is slid upwards to the note on the fifth fret. When playing this example, strike the note a couple of frets lower than the fifth fret and then, without letting any pressure off the string, immediately slide your finger up to the fifth fret.

In the second example, the note is struck and then slid downwards to the lower frets until the string stops sounding. When playing this example, strike the note and then slide down to the lower frets while gradually reducing your finger pressure on the string until the sound stops.

The third example is similar to example 2, except that the slide is upward in direction. When playing this example, strike the note and then slide to the higher frets while gradually reducing your finger pressure on the string until the sound stops.

In the fourth example, the note is struck and then slid to an unspecified higher fret but then reverses direction and slides back down to the lower frets until the string stops sounding. When playing this example, strike the note and then slide to the higher frets. While keeping your finger pressure on the string, reverse direction and slide down to the lower frets as you gradually reduce the finger pressure until the sound stops.

The fifth example is similar to example 4 except that the slides are in opposite directions. When playing this example, strike the note and then slide to the lower frets. While keeping finger pressure on the string, reverse direction and slide to the higher frets as you gradually reduce the pressure until the sound stops.

TRACKS 88–92

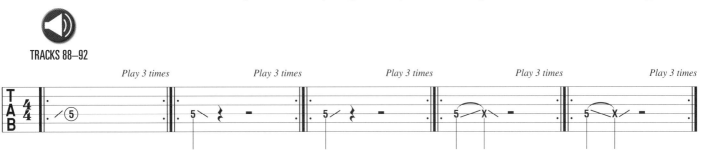

Once you are able to play the examples proficiently, try playing the licks below.

Unmeasured Slide Licks Created from the G Minor Pentatonic Scale:

TRACKS 93–101

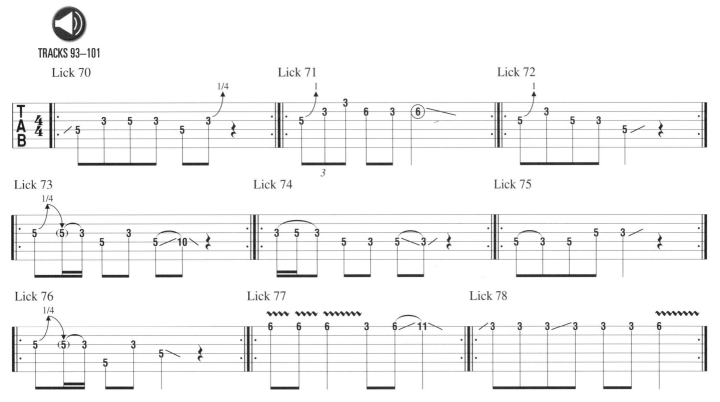

SAMPLE SOLO 3

Shown below is a solo created from the preceding licks and played over Backing Track 3. This solo is more difficult than the first two sample solos—the licks are more challenging and the tempo is faster. The backing track also has a swing feel to it. This track is in the key of B minor, so the licks have been moved up four frets on the fingerboard to accommodate the new key.

TRACK 102

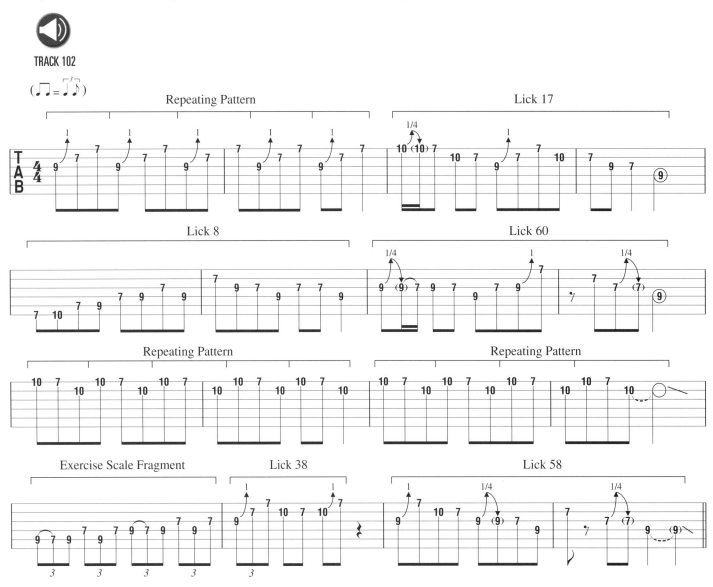

ALTERING A LICK

So far, the sample solos that you've been playing were constructed from one lick being placed after another. Stringing licks together in this fashion is one way to build a solo, but this method can also cause a solo to sound more disjointed because of the many different licks being constantly introduced. In this section, you will learn another way to build your solo and produce more unity at the same time (you will get more mileage out of your licks, too).

The easiest way to create unity in a solo is by repeating a lick. But if the lick is repeated too many times, the solo may get boring. So, instead of repeating the lick exactly the same way, you will slightly alter it on each repetition so that it continually sounds a little different. Introducing a lick and then altering it one or more times gives the listener the best of two worlds: unity and contrast.

Altering a lick can be done in many different ways. In this section, we will examine four different methods. While these methods work better with some licks than they do with others, they are valuable tools to have in your toolbox to use whenever applicable. Let's look at them.

1. CHANGE THE LICK RHYTHMICALLY

With this method, you will be altering a lick by changing it rhythmically. This means changing the time values of the notes in the lick and/or moving the starting point of the lick to different beats of the measure.

Look at the example below. It demonstrates altering a lick by using the first lick that you learned in this book (Lick 1). The example starts with this lick in its original form and then the lick is rhythmically altered six times.

Listen to Track 103 to hear it being played against Backing Track 1. Play along with the audio to get the feel and flow of it. Analyze it to see how the different variations were put together to form a coherent solo using a minimal amount of notes. Then try altering some of the other licks that you've learned, using this method.

TRACK 103

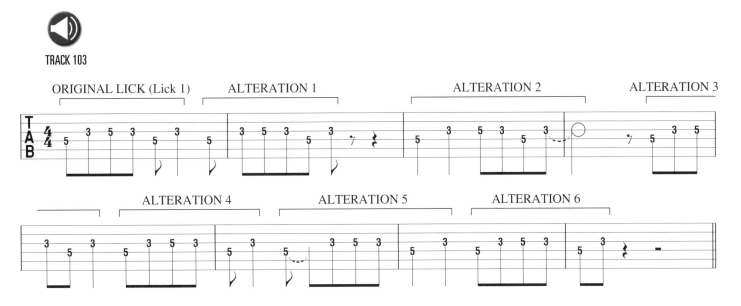

2. REPLACE OR OMIT THE LAST NOTE OF THE LICK

With this method, you will either leave out the last note or replace it with another one. When changing the note, you should replace it with another one from the same scale that was used to create the lick.

Look at the example below, which demonstrates this method. It uses the same lick as the preceding example (Lick 1).

TRACK 104

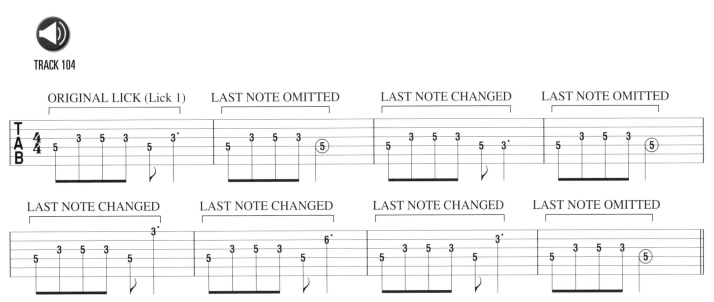

3. ADD NOTES BEFORE OR AFTER THE LICK

With this method, you will place some extra notes before or after the lick. The amount of notes is up to you. Any notes placed after a lick can also be used as a connector, or bridge, to the next lick. Notes that are added should be taken from the same scale that was used to create the lick.

Look at the example below, which demonstrates this method. It uses the same lick as the preceding examples (Lick 1).

TRACK 105

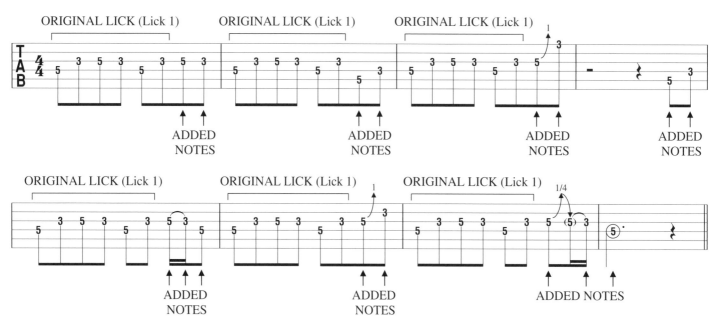

4. REPEAT NOTES IN THE LICK

With this method, you will be repeating various notes of the lick. You'll find here that the repetition of any of the notes will definitely cause the lick to be pushed into different places rhythmically, maybe even into a new measure. Be prepared for some unusual but, hopefully, good results.

Look at the example below, which demonstrates this method. It uses the same lick as the preceding examples (Lick 1).

TRACK 106

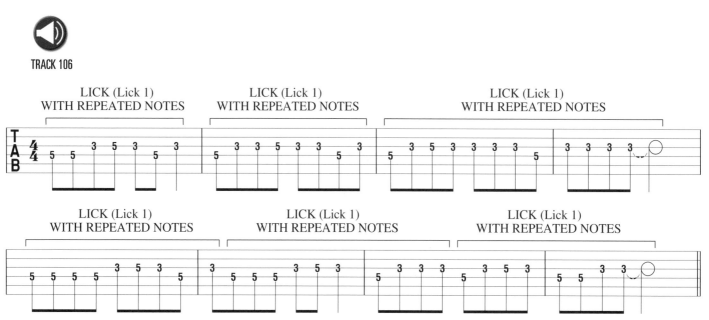

SAMPLE SOLO 4

Shown below is a solo created by using the aforementioned four methods for altering a lick. It is played over Backing Track 1.

TRACK 107

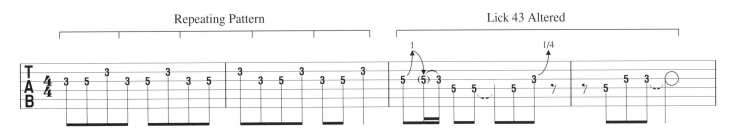

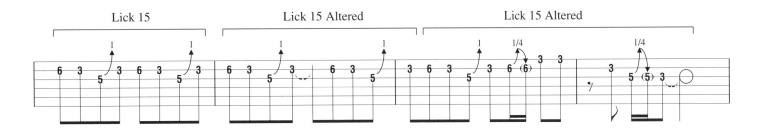

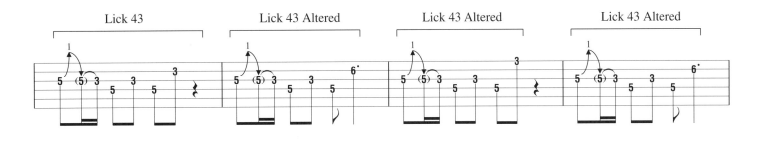

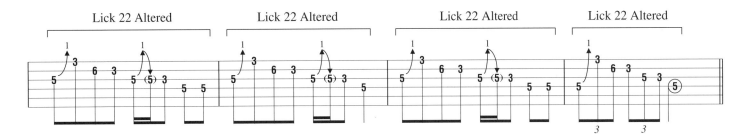

SCALE
THE BLUES SCALE

Shown below is the G blues scale. This scale is similar to the previously learned G minor pentatonic scale, but it has two additional notes known as ♭5ths (black dots). When first starting to use this scale, approach and leave a ♭5th only from the note directly above or below it. For example, in Lick 79, the ♭5th (second note) is approached from the note above and moves to the note below; in Lick 80, the ♭5th (third note) is approached from the note below and moves to the note below; and in Lick 84, the ♭5th (second note) is approached from the note below and moves to the note above. As you gain more familiarity with using the ♭5th, you may try other approaches, such as the ones used in Lick 85 and Lick 86. These notes can be used to make a solo sound more bluesy or melancholy and are typically bent a half step (the half-step bend is explained in a bit).

When soloing, the blues scale and minor pentatonic scale can always be used interchangeably. This will result in added color and diversity. For example, your first lick could be created from the blues scale, the second lick from the minor pentatonic scale, the first half of the third lick could be created from the blues scale, while the second half from the minor pentatonic scale, and so on.

Study and practice the blues scale. Then play the licks that follow.

TRACK 108

G Blues Scale

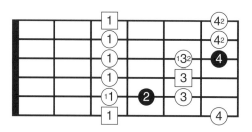

Licks Created from the G Blues Scale:

TRACKS 109–116

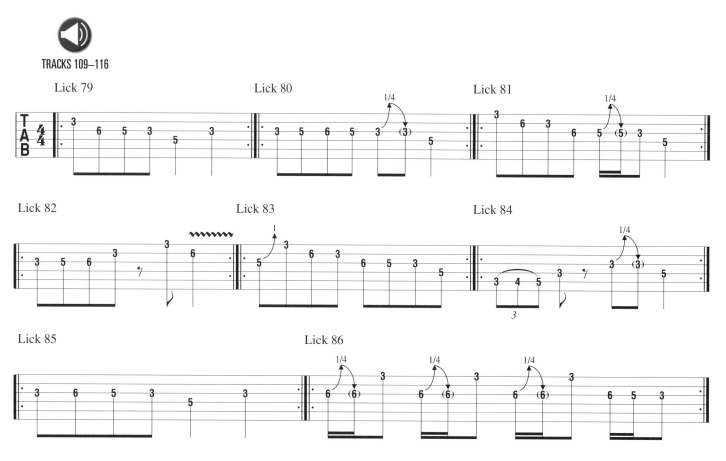

TECHNIQUE
THE HALF-STEP BEND

The *half-step bend* is used with the blues scale because the scale itself has notes that are a half step apart (the minor pentatonic scale does not have any notes a half step apart). There are two notes in this scale that guitarists typically bend a half step and each are located a fret below a ♭5th.

Look at the two examples below. In the first example, the bend is executed with the third finger (like the whole-step bend) to push the string upwards a half step. In contrast, the bend in the second example is executed with the first finger to pull the string downwards a half step. If you need to check the pitch accuracy of a bent string, play the unbent note one fret higher.

Try playing the examples below. Once you are able to play them proficiently, try playing the licks that follow.

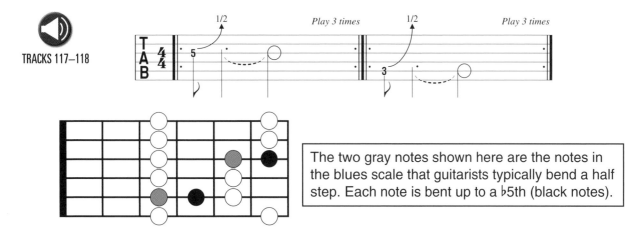

TRACKS 117–118

The two gray notes shown here are the notes in the blues scale that guitarists typically bend a half step. Each note is bent up to a ♭5th (black notes).

Half-Step Bend Licks Created from the G Blues Scale:

TRACKS 119–126

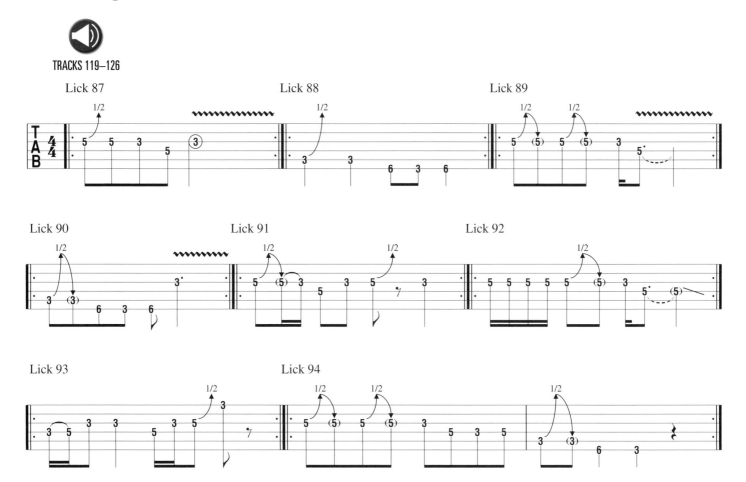

THE UNISON BEND

The *unison bend* is a technique involving two strings that are struck simultaneously, with one of the strings being bent a whole step. The unison bend can be played on either the first and second strings or the second and third strings.

This technique is executed almost the same way as the whole-step bends from earlier. Look at the two examples below. Instead of bending the first note (here, on string 3) up a whole step and then striking the next string (shown on the left side of each example), both strings are struck simultaneously (shown on the right side of each example).

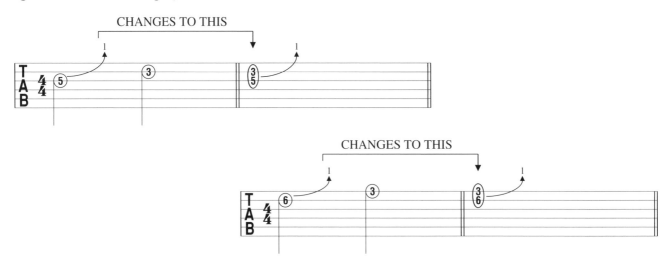

Now look at the third example, shown below. This example shows the highest four notes of the G minor pentatonic scale played as unison bends. Try playing the example. The proper fingerings for these bends are shown below the tab.

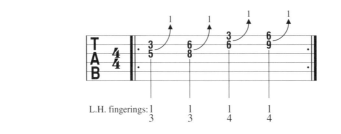

TRACK 127

Once you are able to play this proficiently, try playing the licks that follow.

Unison Bend Licks Created from the G Minor Pentatonic Scale:

TRACKS 128–133

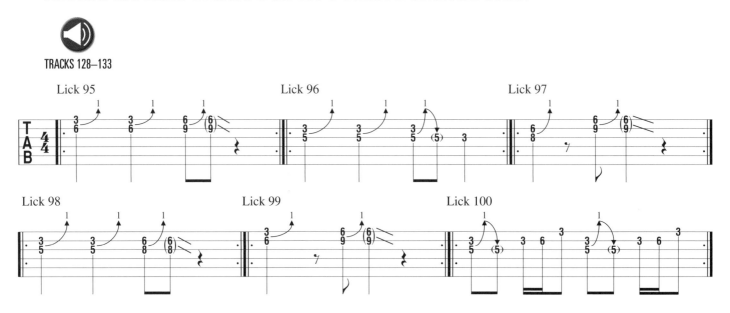

DOUBLE STOPS

Guitarists will sometimes play two different notes at the same time. Two different notes played simultaneously are called *double stops*. While any two notes of the minor pentatonic scale can be played together with good results, the most commonly used double stops are ones created from three different scales: the minor pentatonic scale, the blues scale, and the Dorian mode (the Dorian mode will be studied in Part II).

Shown below are these double stops grouped together to form a composite set that can be easily played. As you can see, one finger can be used to depress both notes of each double stop. Try playing them. Then try playing the licks that follow.

TRACK 134

Composite set of popular double stops used with the G minor pentatonic or blues scales

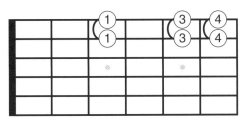

Licks Using Double Stops (Use These with the G Minor Pentatonic or G Blues Scales):

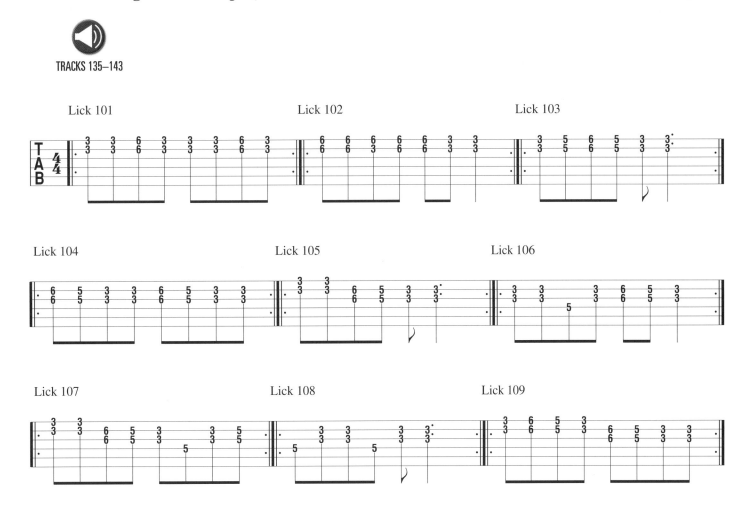

MEASURED SLIDES

The *measured slide* is a slide that begins and ends on a specific fret. There are two types of measured slides: the *legato slide* and the *shift slide*. The difference between the two is that the note being slid to is struck in the shift slide but not in the legato slide.

Look below at the legato slides in the first two examples. In these examples, the first note is struck and then slid to the second note. The only difference between the two examples is that the slide goes upwards in the first example and downwards in the second.

Now look at the shift slides shown in the third and fourth examples. In these examples, the first note is struck and then slid to the second note, which is also struck. The second note is usually played immediately after the slide, but there can be an appreciable amount of time before actually starting the slide. Like the first two examples, the difference between these two examples is the direction of the slides.

The correct finger to use for a measured slide should be the one normally used for the second note of the slide. Since these examples were created from the G minor pentatonic scale, you should use the third finger for the notes in examples 1 and 3 and the first finger for the notes in examples 2 and 4.

Try playing the examples. Once you are able to play them proficiently, try playing the licks that follow.

TRACKS 144–147

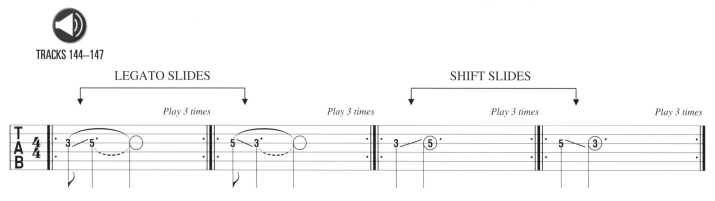

Legato Slide and Shift Slide Licks Created from the G Minor Pentatonic Scale:

TRACKS 148–156

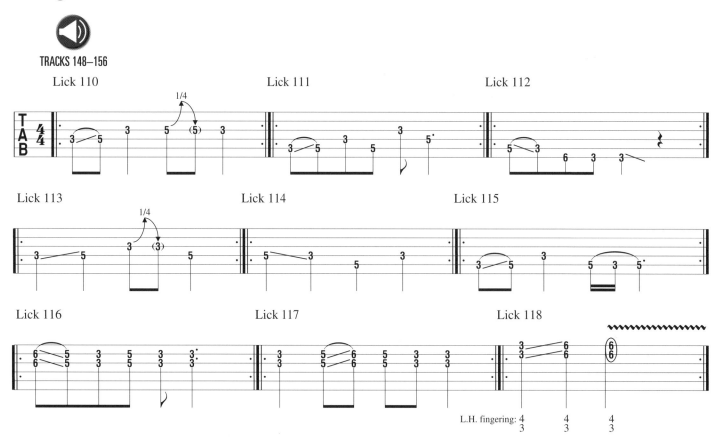

SAMPLE SOLO 5

Shown below is a solo created from previously learned licks and played over Backing Track 5. This track is in the key of A minor, so the G minor pentatonic/blues licks have been moved up two frets on the fingerboard to accommodate this key. Try creating your own solo over the backing track using the A minor pentatonic and A blues scales.

TRACK 157

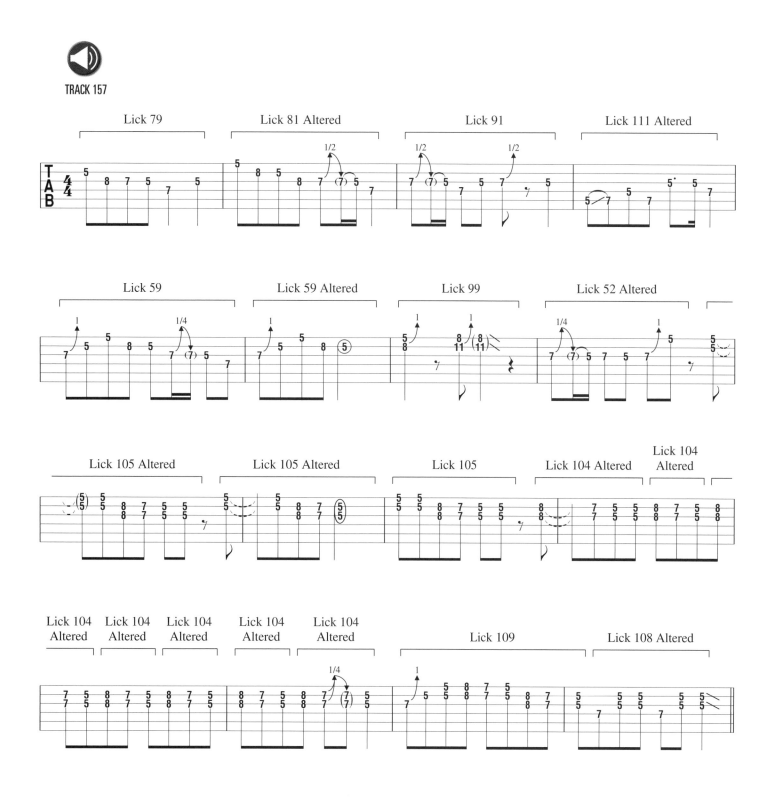

SCALE
THE EXTENDED MINOR PENTATONIC SCALE

Shown below is the extended G minor pentatonic scale. This is an alternate form of the standard G minor pentatonic scale, with a slightly higher and lower range of notes.

Notice that there is one note in this formation that guitarists typically bend a whole step. Also notice the note with an arrow pointing to it: when trying to make certain licks in the higher range of the scale easier to play, this note is often played with the second finger (a change in fingering will be indicated under the tab).

Practice the scale. Then play the licks shown below.

TRACK 158

Extended G Minor Pentatonic Scale

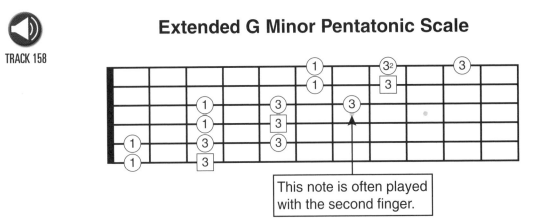

This note is often played with the second finger.

Licks Created from the Extended G Minor Pentatonic Scale:

TRACKS 159–166

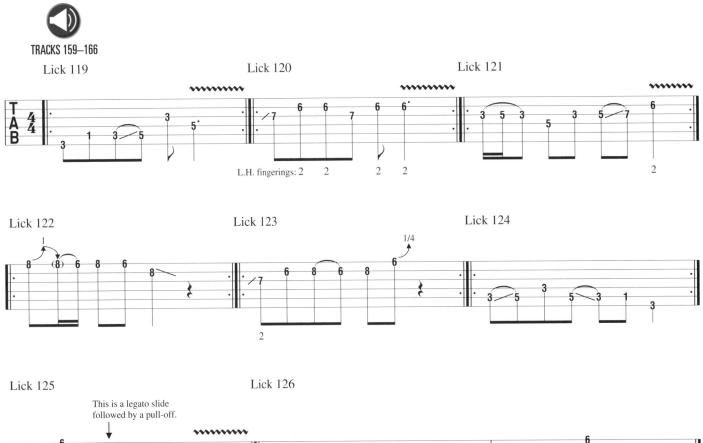

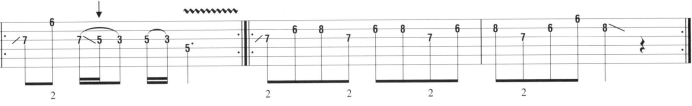

34   *Guitar Soloing Basics*

TECHNIQUE
FIRST FINGER WHOLE-STEP BENDS

So far, you have only performed whole-step bends with your third or fourth finger. In this section, you'll learn two whole-step bends that are executed with the first finger. Unlike the previously learned whole-step bends, these are much more difficult to play because you don't have an extra finger to help push the string upwards. They will, however, be easier to execute when moving the scale to the higher frets because of the lessened string tension involved.

Look at the two examples below. Each one shows a first finger whole-step bend taken from the extended G minor pentatonic scale. When playing the first example, the first finger can either push the string upwards or pull it down a whole step. When playing the second example, the first finger must push the string upwards a whole step because the reverse direction will cause the string to slip off the fingerboard.

Try playing the examples:

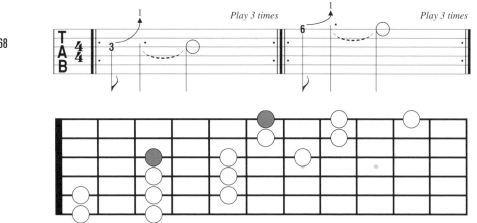

TRACKS 167–168

The two gray notes shown here are the notes that guitarists typically bend a whole step with the first finger.

Once you are able to play the two examples proficiently, try playing the licks shown below.

First Finger Whole-Step Bend Licks Created from the Extended G Minor Pentatonic Scale:

TRACKS 169–174

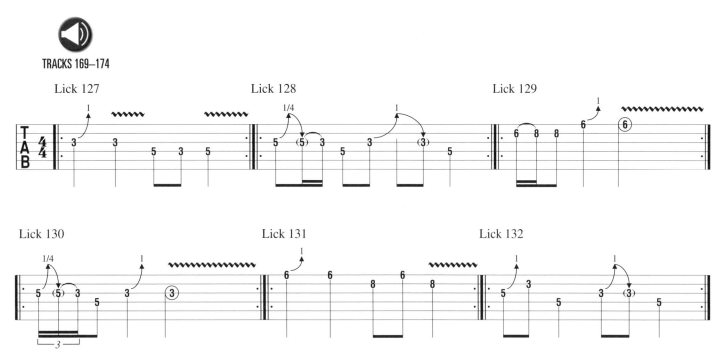

TECHNIQUE
CONNECTING SCALES

Guitarists will sometimes play licks created from both the regular and the extended forms of the minor pentatonic scale. Licks using both forms of the scale are often linked together with the legato slide.

Look below at the five examples using the legato slide to connect the G minor pentatonic scale with the extended G minor pentatonic scale. The first three examples use the technique to go upwards from the regular form to the extended form of the scale. The fourth and fifth examples use the technique to go downwards from the extended form to the regular form of the scale. The fingerings are included below the tab for all of the notes to ensure that you use the correct scale formation.

Try playing the examples. Once you are able to play them proficiently, try playing the licks that follow.

TRACKS 175–179

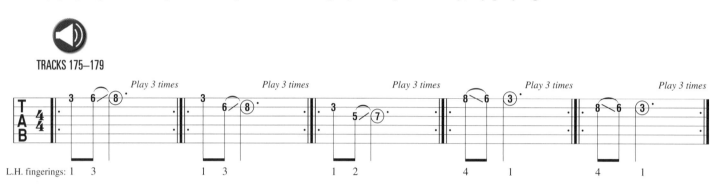

Licks Using the Legato Slide to Connect the G Minor Pentatonic Scale to the Extended G Minor Pentatonic Scale:

TRACKS 180–187

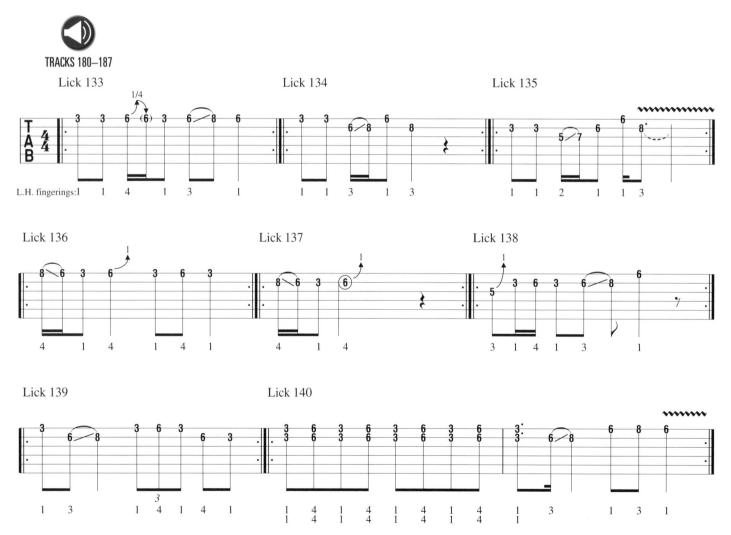

EXERCISES USING THE EXTENDED MINOR PENTATONIC SCALE

Exercises Created from the Extended G Minor Pentatonic Scale:

TRACKS 188–191

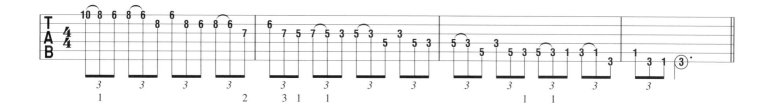

THE PRE-BEND

Shown below are two examples using a technique called the *pre-bend*. This technique is executed by bending a note and then striking it. In other words, the string is struck *after* the bend has already taken place.

The pre-bend is shown in the first example below and indicated by a vertical arrow with the bending distance number above it. The pre-bend with release is shown in the second example and indicated similarly to example 1, except that the arrow turns back downwards (the release). Try playing both examples.

TRACKS 192–193

Once you are able to play the above examples proficiently, try playing the licks below.

Licks Using the Pre-Bend—Licks 141–145 Created from the G Minor Pentatonic Scale; Licks 146–149 Created from the Extended G Minor Pentatonic Scale:

TRACKS 194–202

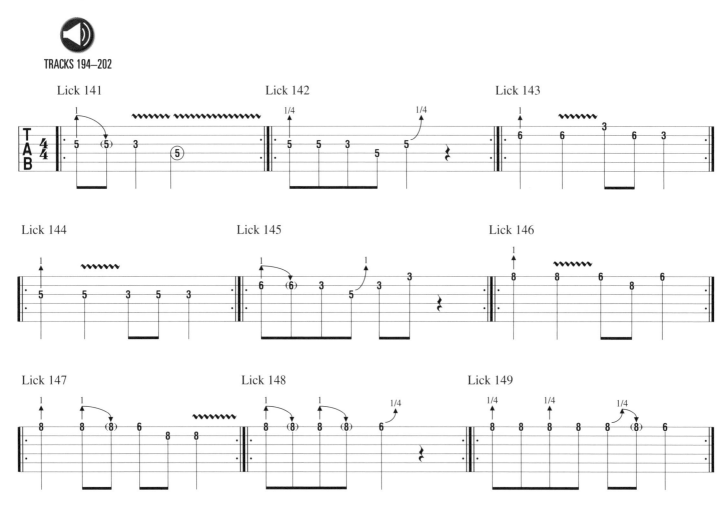

TECHNIQUE
MORE BENDS WITH ONE NOTE

The two examples shown below are a couple of popular bends executed on one note of the extended G minor pentatonic scale. Below the two examples is a fingerboard diagram showing where the note is located in the scale formation.

In the first example, the note is bent a whole step. This is different from any of the previously learned bends because here the string is being bent to a note that is *not* in the scale. Try playing the example. In order to check if the pitch of the bent note is correct, play the note (unbent) two frets higher (10th fret).

In the second example, the note is bent one-and-a-half steps. Bending a string one-and-a-half steps is the maximum extent of most guitarists' bending ability. Try playing the example. In order to check if the pitch of the bent note is correct, play the note (unbent) three frets higher (eleventh fret).

Once you are able to play both examples proficiently, try playing the licks that follow.

TRACKS 203–204

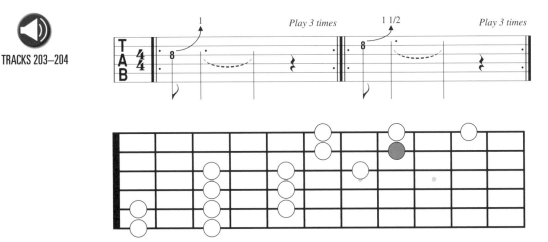

The gray note is typically bent either a whole step or one-and-a-half steps and is located in the extended minor pentatonic scale.

Whole-Step and One-and-a-Half-Step Bends Created from the Extended G Minor Pentatonic Scale:

TRACKS 205–210

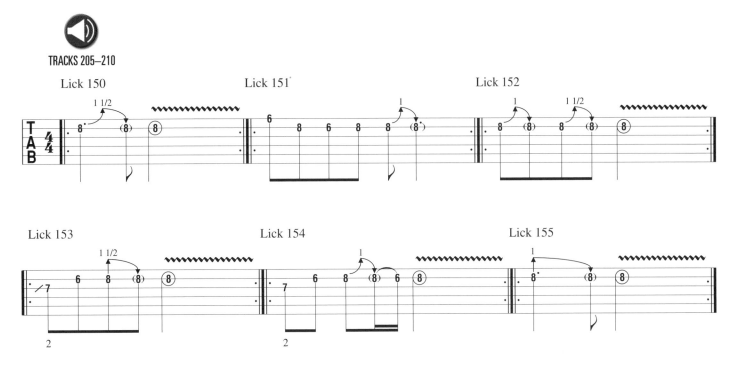

THE DOUBLE-STOP BEND

Shown below is a technique called the *double-stop bend*. This technique involves the simultaneous bending of two strings using one of the previously learned double stops.

The example below shows a previously learned double stop, with two bend arrows added to each string—the bottom note being bent a whole step and the top note only a half step. This technique may look daunting at first, but it is easier to play than you might imagine.

There are two ways to execute this double stop bend: one method is to push the strings upwards to their proper pitches, using the third finger on the bottom note and the fourth finger on the top note. The other method is to pull the strings downward to their proper pitches, using your third finger on both notes. Try playing the example with both fingering options to see which one works best for you.

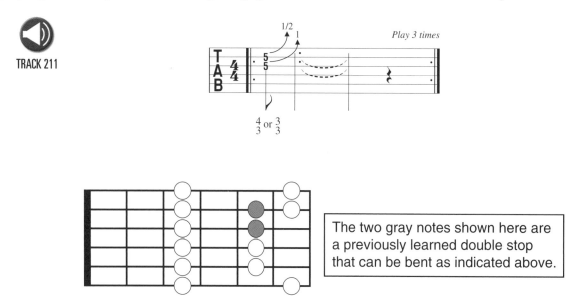

The two gray notes shown here are a previously learned double stop that can be bent as indicated above.

Once you are able to play the example proficiently, try playing the licks below.

Double-Stop Bend Licks—Use These with the G Minor Pentatonic Scale or G Blues Scale:

TRACKS 212–217

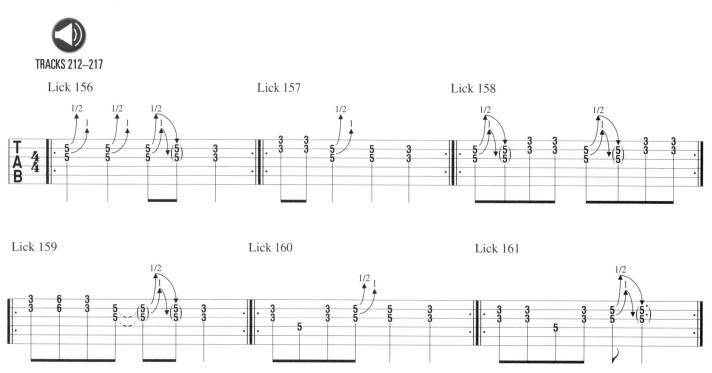

SAMPLE SOLO 6

Shown below is a solo created from licks on the preceding pages and played over Backing Track 8. This track is in the key of G minor. Parts of the solo may seem reminiscent of the classic solo in Led Zeppelin's song "Stairway to Heaven."

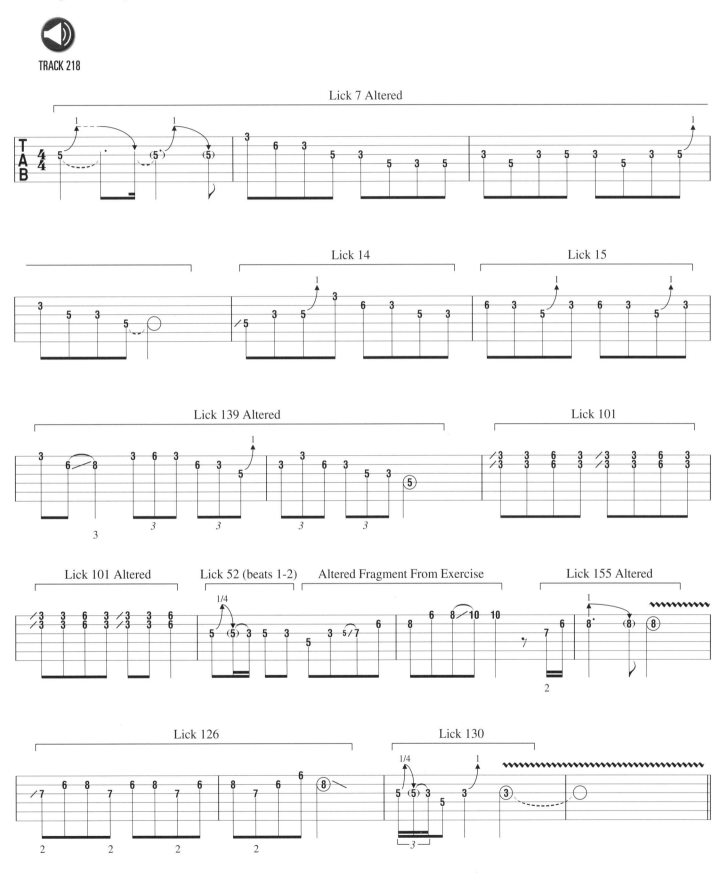

TRACK 218

SCALE
THE EXTENDED BLUES SCALE

Shown below is the extended G blues scale. It is similar to the extended G minor pentatonic scale except that there are some ♭5ths (black dots) added. Notice that there is one note on the first string of the scale that guitarists typically bend either a half step or a whole step.

Practice the scale. Then play the licks shown below.

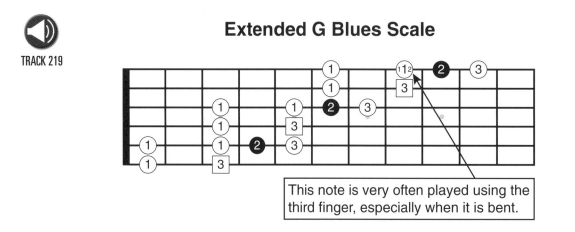

TRACK 219

Extended G Blues Scale

This note is very often played using the third finger, especially when it is bent.

Licks Created from the Extended G Blues Scale:

TRACKS 220–227

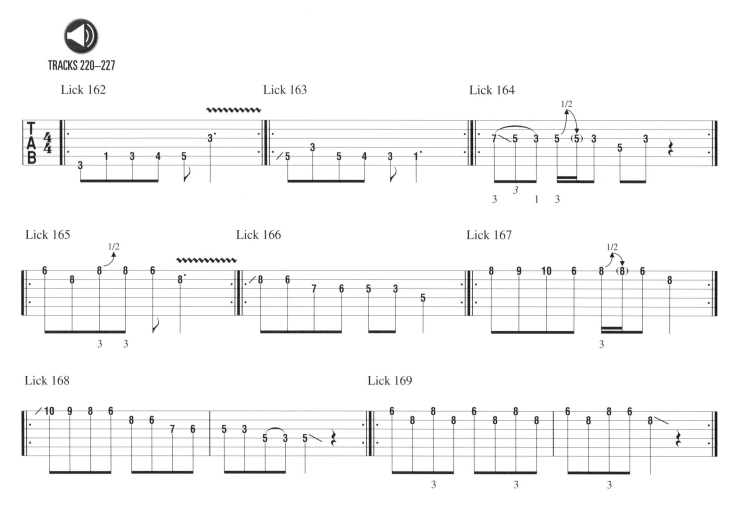

THE MAJOR PENTATONIC SCALES

Shown below are two more types of pentatonic scales: the B♭ major pentatonic scale and the B♭ major pentatonic scale with ♭3rd. These scales have a happier sound when compared to the other scales that you've been playing. The major pentatonic scales can be used interchangeably for soloing like you did with the minor pentatonic scale and blues scale.

Look at the B♭ major pentatonic scale. It is similar to the G minor pentatonic scale except the tonic is now the second note of the formation, B♭. Consequently, since the tonic is now B♭, the letter name of the scale has been changed to that note.

Now look at the B♭ major pentatonic scale with ♭3rd (for best results, the ♭3rds [black dots] should be treated like the ♭5ths in the blues scale). It is similar to the G blues scale except the tonic is now the second note of the formation, B♭. And since the tonic is now B♭, the letter name of the scale has been changed to that note.

For the purpose of this book, we will call any two identically configured scales having different names and tonic locations as *form-equivalent scales*. Thus, the G minor pentatonic scale is form-equivalent to the B♭ major pentatonic scale, and the G blues scale is form-equivalent to the B♭ major pentatonic scale with ♭3rd. Form-equivalent scales will be discussed more in a bit.

Study these scales and then go to the extended forms of these scales that follow.

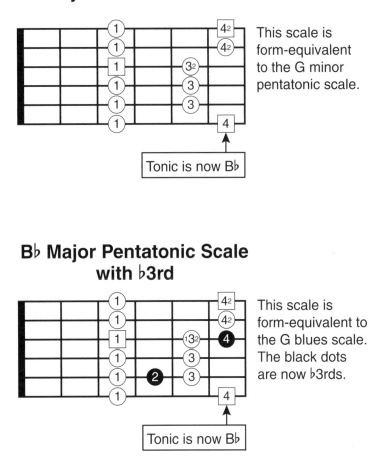

B♭ Major Pentatonic Scale

This scale is form-equivalent to the G minor pentatonic scale.

Tonic is now B♭

B♭ Major Pentatonic Scale with ♭3rd

This scale is form-equivalent to the G blues scale. The black dots are now ♭3rds.

Tonic is now B♭

THE EXTENDED MAJOR PENTATONIC SCALES

Shown below is the extended B♭ major pentatonic scale. It is form-equivalent to the extended G minor pentatonic scale.

Notice that the two bends on the second string of the extended minor pentatonic scale are not included in the extended major pentatonic scale. They are not typical bends for this scale.

Study and practice the scale.

Extended B♭ Major Pentatonic Scale

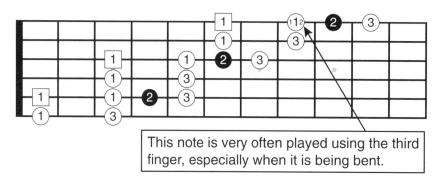

Here is the extended B♭ major pentatonic scale with ♭3rd. It is form-equivalent to the extended G blues scale.

Study and practice the scale.

Extended B♭ Major Pentatonic Scale with ♭3rd

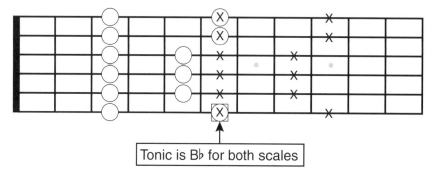

This note is very often played using the third finger, especially when it is being bent.

MORE ABOUT FORM-EQUIVALENT SCALES

You may be asking, "Why are two form-equivalent scales regarded as two different scales with two different names when they both have the same notes?" The answer can be seen when you move the two scales to the same key.

Look at the fingerboard diagram below, which shows the B♭ major pentatonic scale (represented by the circles) and the B♭ minor pentatonic scale (represented by the Xs). What can be seen are two scales with the same formation and the same tonic. However, they are in different locations on the fingerboard, so they actually do have different notes. Therefore, they are actually two different scales!

Tonic is B♭ for both scales

LICKS AND FORM-EQUIVALENT SCALES

Now you know that one formation of notes can be regarded as two different scales. In similar fashion, the licks that you've learned and you know as being created from one particular scale can now be seen as being created from two different scales. Consequently, the number of licks that you know has just doubled!

In order to use your licks with a form-equivalent scale, the letter and scale name of the scale that was used to create the licks needs to be converted to the letter and scale name of the form-equivalent scale (licks that use double stops and/or certain bends cannot be converted).

Use the guide below to convert the licks that you have learned:

- G Minor Pentatonic Scale Created Licks = B♭ Major Pentatonic Scale Licks

- G Blues Scale Created Licks = B♭ Major Pentatonic Scale with ♭3rd Licks

Now try converting the licks that you've learned and play them over the appropriate backing tracks. When used in an actual soloing context, the converted licks should have a much more happy sound to them in comparison.

EFFECTIVE SOLOING

DETERMINING THE CORRECT SCALES TO USE

In order to solo effectively, you'll need to know the specific scales that can be used for a solo. You already know that a scale (or licks created from a scale) should be in the same key as the music. You also know that keys have either a major or minor quality. However, you might not know that scales also have a major or minor quality (there are other scale qualities, as well, but that is not relevant here). And determining if a scale can be used for a solo first requires knowing the major or minor quality of the scale, as well as if that quality is compatible with the major or minor quality of the key.

Look at the diagram below:

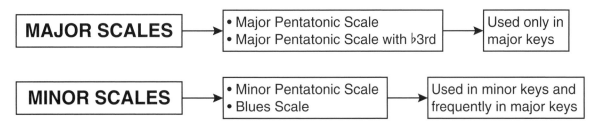

From this diagram, you can see that the major pentatonic scale and the major pentatonic scale with ♭3rd are both major scales, whereas the minor pentatonic scale and the blues scale are both minor scales. You can also see that the major scales are only used in major keys, whereas the minor scales are not only used in minor keys, but frequently in major keys, too. The only time a minor scale should not be used in a major key is when it sounds too discordant against the chords being soloed over.

For example, when using the above information, if you were in the key of F major, you could use any of the major or minor scales; however, if the minor scales sound too discordant, you should play the major scales exclusively. In contrast, if you were in the key of F minor, you should use only the minor scales.

DETERMINING THE KEY

Guitarists who are well-versed in music theory should have no problem determining the key of the music. For others, the method shown below can usually be relied upon. To understand this method, first look at these features of the *tonic chord*: the tonic chord has the same letter name and major or minor quality as the key. For example, the tonic chord in the key of C is a C chord, and the tonic chord in the key of A minor is an Am chord. Now look below at the method for determining the key.

The Tonic Chord Is Usually the First Chord in the Progression You Are Soloing Over

Let's apply this information: if you are soloing over a chord progression that has an F♯ major for its first chord, the key is probably F♯ major. If the first chord is an F♯ minor, the key is probably F♯ minor. If the first chord is an F power chord (power chords are neither major nor minor), try the key of F minor, but switch to F major if the notes don't sound right.

If the notes still do not sound right after you've followed the above method, the first chord probably isn't the tonic chord, which means that you're soloing in the wrong key. In such cases, you must experiment by playing the scales in different places on the fingerboard until the notes do sound right. This process may be slow and difficult at first, but it will get better as your ears become more developed.

SAMPLE SOLO 7

Here is a more robust solo in the key of B♭ major and played over Backing Track 7. It uses the B♭ major pentatonic scale and incorporates licks originally created from the G minor pentatonic scale, its form-equivalent scale. Notice that some altered licks are more extreme. There is also some "free material," which is ad-libbed material created from the B♭ major pentatonic scale to fill the space between licks. This track (Track 228) is in cut time and has a two-measure (four-beat) starting click.

TRACK 228

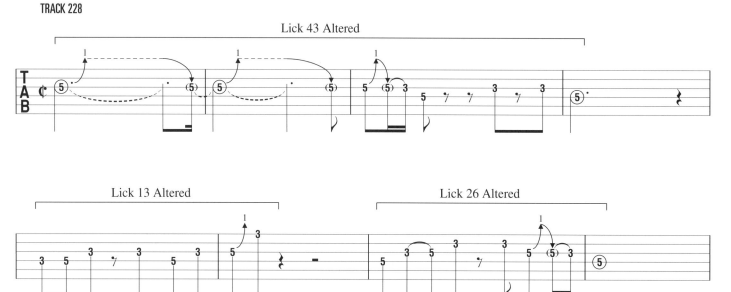

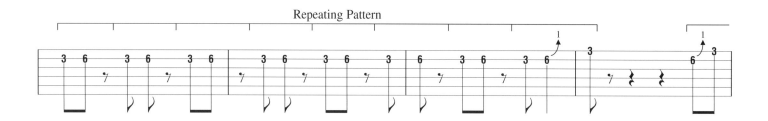

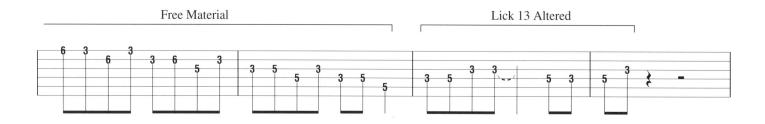

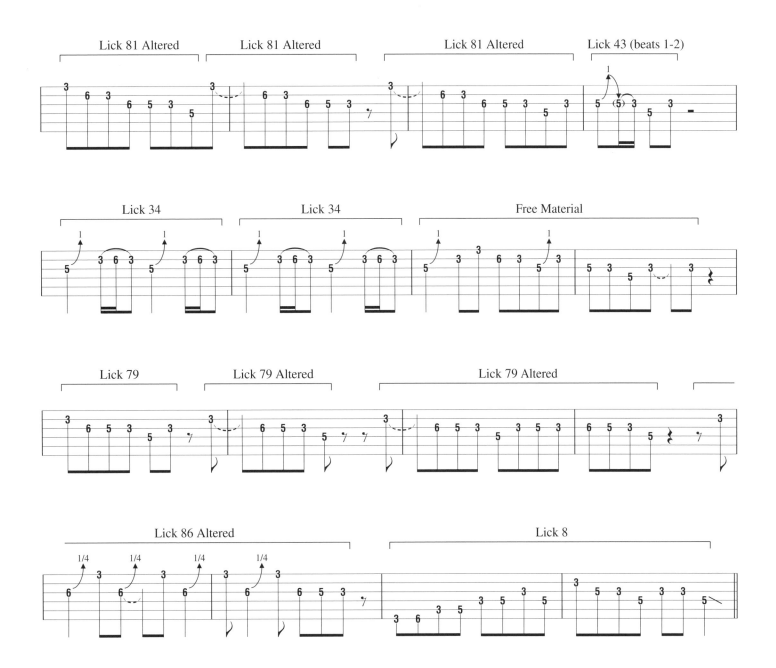

By now, you should have a good idea of how a solo can be constructed by using unaltered and altered licks. Although you are probably putting some real forethought into your own solo construction, an experienced soloist can put together an entire solo without being too conscious of the actual mechanics taking place.

But you, too, will eventually get to that point! Just continue creating your own licks and experimenting with the ones you've already learned—connect them, alter them, throw in some repeating patterns, and so on. The more you work at creating your own solos, the more you'll find them flowing from you without any apparent effort!

Don't forget about including emotion in your playing, either. For example, give your notes more feeling by playing some of them softly and others more loudly, or grow louder when you want to come to a peak in your solo. If you want to create a frenzy, make your playing busier by gradually adding more notes of diminishing time values. Talk to your listeners through your solos, as if you were trying to convince them of something with real conviction and passion—don't end up being a machine that coldly spews out one lick after another. Integrating your soul into your solos can make a real difference in how well the solos are accepted by the listener.

SAMPLE SOLO 8

This solo demonstrates the use of both the major pentatonic and the minor pentatonic scale in the same major key. It also shows how the same lick can be used in both scales; for example, the first measure is the same lick as the second measure, except the former is played in the minor pentatonic scale and the latter in the major pentatonic. This back and forth between a minor and major lick continues throughout the solo. The solo is played over Backing Track 6 and is in the key of B♭ major.

TRACK 229

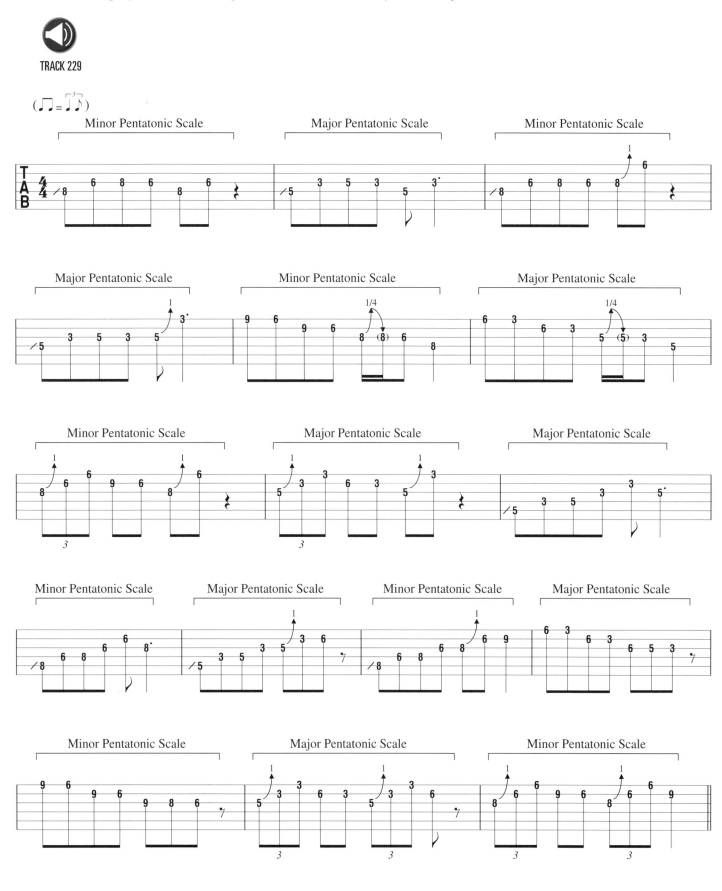

SCALE
THE HYBRID MAJOR PENTATONIC SCALE

Shown below is the hybrid F major pentatonic scale. This scale is actually another extended form of the major pentatonic scale, with four more notes added to its higher register, as shown by the arrows. Many well-known licks have been created with this higher-register version of the scale.

Familiarize yourself with the scale—the black note is a ♭5th. Try playing the scale and then the licks that follow. You can also try playing the scale without the four added notes, thus making it another extended form of the F major pentatonic scale.

TRACK 230

Hybrid F Major Pentatonic Scale

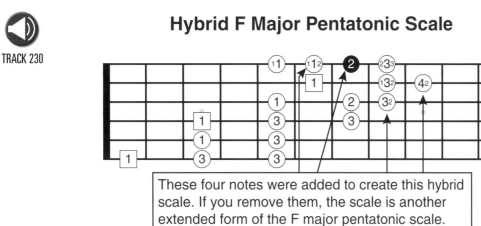

These four notes were added to create this hybrid scale. If you remove them, the scale is another extended form of the F major pentatonic scale.

Licks Created from the Hybrid F Major Pentatonic Scale:

TRACKS 231–239

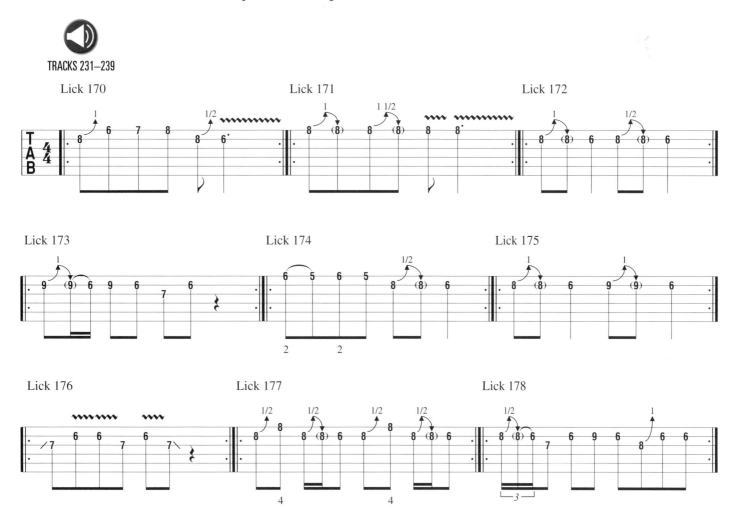

SAMPLE SOLO 9

Shown below is a solo created from the aforementioned hybrid major pentatonic scale. It is played over Backing Track 4, which is another 12-bar blues but with a swing feel. Because this track is in the key of C major, the licks have been moved up seven frets to accommodate the new key.

The style of this solo is reminiscent of blues guitarist B.B. King, but you could easily adapt it to a rock style and play it in the solo section of a song such as Lynyrd Skynyrd's "Free Bird." ("Free Bird" is in the key of G major, with a straight-eighth feel to it.)

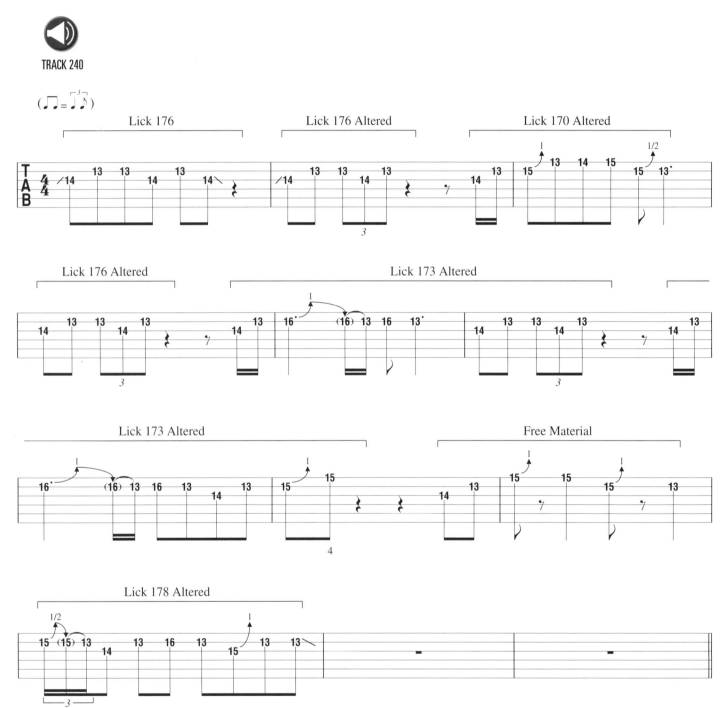

TRACK 240

PART II

In Part II, you will continue your study of soloing by learning some more scales: the *modes*. Although not used as often as the scales presented in Part I, the modes are invaluable because they can give solos an interesting edge due to their unique sound qualities.

You will also learn the *Phrygian dominant scale*. This scale is more difficult to play, physically, but it will lend a truly exotic quality to your solos. After hearing it, you will probably agree that it has the most easily recognizable sound of any scale in this book.

Study Part II thoroughly. When completed, you will have learned all of the scales used for soloing by guitarists in popular music. This is a giant step towards becoming a master soloist!

THE MODES

Shown on the following pages are seven scales called *modes* (the modes originated in Greece long ago but still retain their Greek names). The fingerings and small bend numbers are not included in the diagrams but will be shown when each mode is studied individually on the pages that follow.

Notice that there are two sets of three modes, each grouped according to their major or minor quality. To the far right of the diagrams is the frequency that each mode is used by blues-based guitarists. The Locrian mode is never really used, so it will not be studied. (The Locrian mode is commonly employed by jazz guitarists for playing over half-diminished chords.)

Also notice that a major or minor pentatonic scale, indicated by the white circles and squares, resides within each mode. If you think of a mode as being a pentatonic scale with some added notes (indicated by the gray circles), it may be easier to memorize and use.

Finally, pay close attention to the differences between the notes of each mode within each group. For example, there isn't much difference between the Aeolian and Dorian modes or the Aeolian and Phrygian modes. Being able to discern these slight differences will make memorizing them easier and help when trying to find the better mode to use for a solo.

FINDING THE BETTER MODE TO USE FOR SOLOING

As a starting point, you should use a major mode when in a major key, and a minor mode when in a minor key. However, there is one mode from each major and minor group that will sound better than another, depending on the chords being soloed over. Follow these directions to determine the better mode:

First, assume that the better mode is the Ionian mode when in a major key, and the Aeolian mode is the better mode when in a minor key. Then determine if the notes making up each mode are contained in the chords that you will be soloing over. If they aren't, you must find the mode that does have them (you can use the fingerboard diagram on page 6 to help identify the notes contained in the chords and modes).

For example, let's say you want to solo over Em and C chords in the key of E minor. First, assume that the E Aeolian mode is the better mode to use. Then compare the notes in the Em and C chords with the notes in the mode (see below). Because the Aeolian mode has all of the notes in these two chords, it is the better mode to use. If you were soloing over Em and A chords, then the Dorian mode would be a better choice because it has the C♯ note that's found in the A chord.

Em Chord: E–G–B   E Aeolian Mode: E–F♯–G–A–B–C–D
C Chord: C–E–G   E MINOR MODES {   E Dorian Mode: E–F♯–G–A–B–C♯–D
A Chord: A–C♯–E   E Phrygian Mode: E–F–G–A–B–C–D

If the above method is too difficult, try using your ear to find the better mode: while listening to the chords, play the notes in each mode that are different from one another. Observe which modes contain the notes that clash the most and then eliminate them as a choice. Eventually, you'll be left with the better mode.

For example, if you are soloing over Em and A chords in the key of E minor, the C♯ note in the A chord will clash with the C natural note in the Aeolian and Phrygian modes. However, since the Dorian mode has the C♯ note in it, there won't be any clash of notes; therefore, the Dorian mode will be the better mode to use. (While you do not have to know the letter names of the notes when using this method, you must be able to discern if the notes you play fit well, aurally, over the chords being played.)

Study the diagrams. Then proceed to the following pages to examine the modes individually.

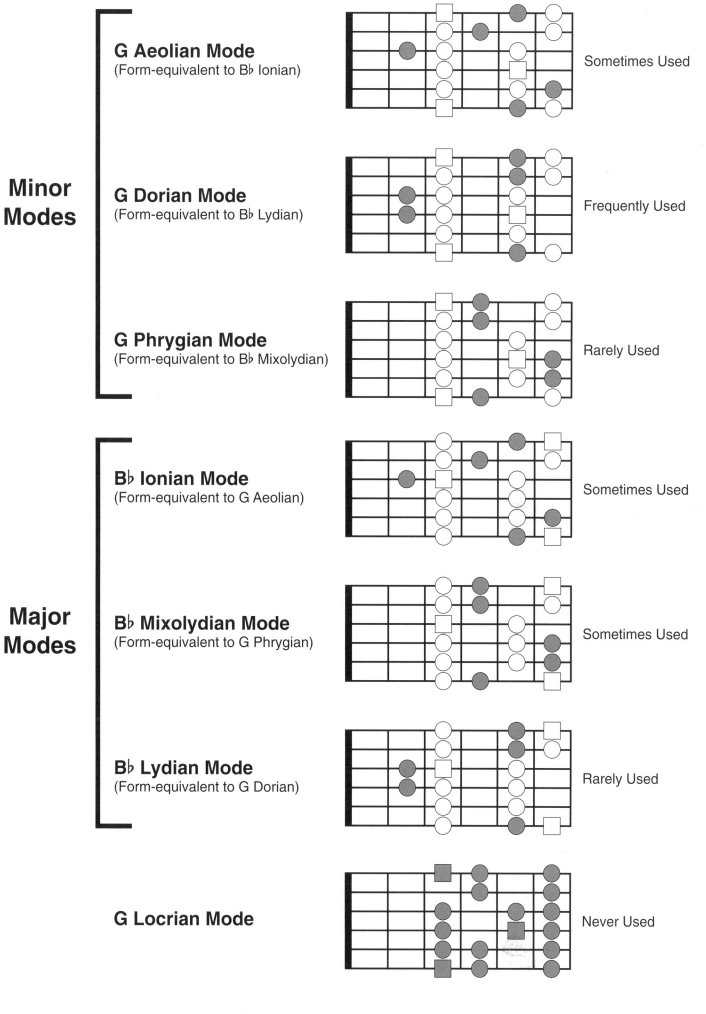

Minor Modes

G Aeolian Mode
(Form-equivalent to Bb Ionian)

Sometimes Used

G Dorian Mode
(Form-equivalent to Bb Lydian)

Frequently Used

G Phrygian Mode
(Form-equivalent to Bb Mixolydian)

Rarely Used

Major Modes

Bb Ionian Mode
(Form-equivalent to G Aeolian)

Sometimes Used

Bb Mixolydian Mode
(Form-equivalent to G Phrygian)

Sometimes Used

Bb Lydian Mode
(Form-equivalent to G Dorian)

Rarely Used

G Locrian Mode

Never Used

SCALE
THE AEOLIAN MODE

The Aeolian mode (also called the "natural minor scale") is a minor mode. It sounds sadder than the Dorian mode, but not as sad as the Phrygian mode.

Shown below is the G Aeolian mode. Try to discern the G minor pentatonic scale residing in the mode, because it will make the mode easier to remember and use. The note with the arrow pointing to it is often played with the third finger when being bent (the same finger used for bending the note in the G minor pentatonic scale).

Study this mode and then practice playing it. Then play the licks that follow.

TRACK 241

G Aeolian Mode
(Natural Minor Scale)

The third finger is often used to bend this note.

Licks Created from the G Aeolian Mode:

TRACKS 242–249

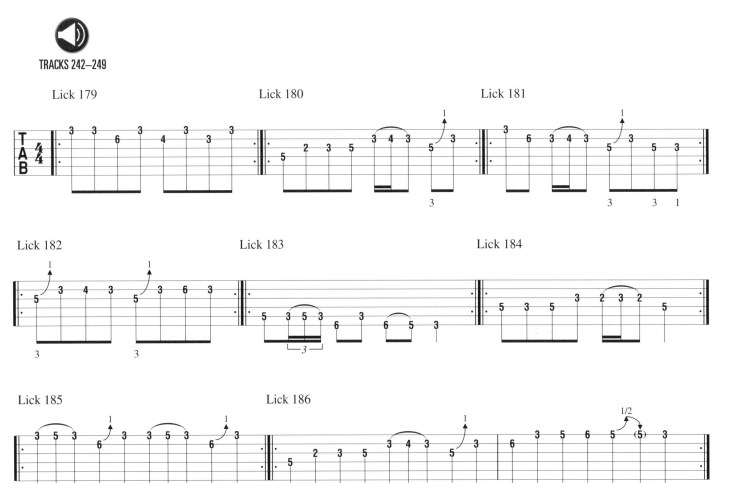

SAMPLE SOLO 10

This solo demonstrates the use of the G Aeolian mode and is played over Backing Track 8.

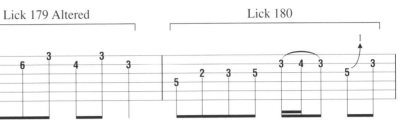

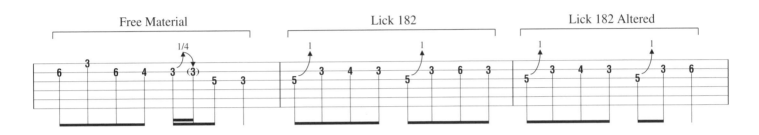

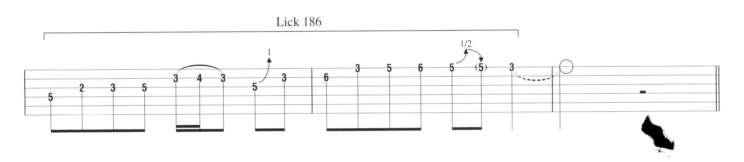

THE DORIAN MODE

The Dorian mode is the most used mode of blues-based guitarists. It is a minor mode but, like the minor pentatonic scale and blues scale, it is frequently used in major keys. The Dorian mode sounds the least sad of the minor modes.

Shown below is the G Dorian mode. As before, try to discern the G minor pentatonic scale residing in the mode. The note with the arrow pointing to it is often played with the third finger when being bent (the same finger used for bending the note in the G minor pentatonic scale).

Study this mode and then practice playing it. Then play the licks that follow.

TRACK 251

G Dorian Mode
(Minor Mode)

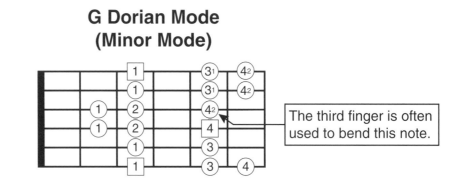

The third finger is often used to bend this note.

Licks Created from the G Dorian Mode:

TRACKS 252–259

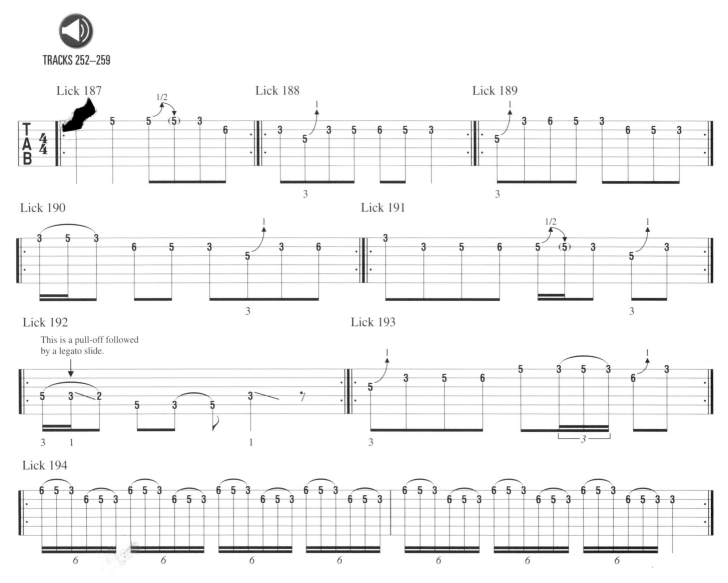

SAMPLE SOLO 11

Shown below is a solo created mainly from the G Dorian mode. As previously noted, this mode is used frequently in major keys even though it is really a minor mode. The solo is played over Backing Track 2 in the key of G major.

Notice that although the Dorian mode is the predominant scale being used, the blues scale is also used (measure 4), as are some double stops. This is common practice among guitarists when playing old rock 'n' roll or blues music, which this track emulates.

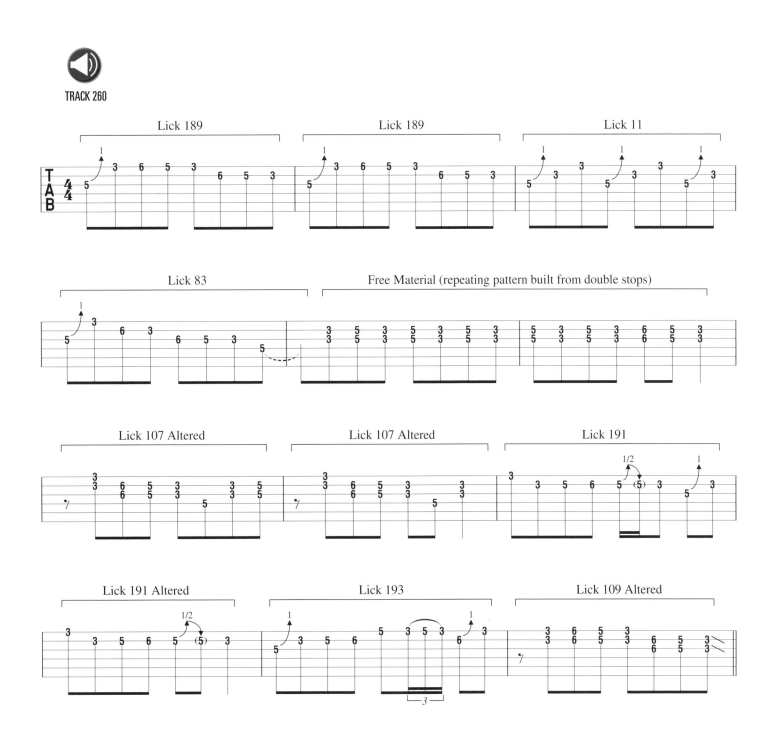

TRACK 260

THE PHRYGIAN MODE

The Phrygian mode is the last of the three minor modes and has the saddest sound quality. Although rarely used by blues-based guitarists, the fingering for this mode is easy to master because the fingerboard span encompasses only four frets as opposed to five frets like the other two minor modes.

Shown below is the G Phrygian mode. As before, try to discern the G minor pentatonic scale residing in the mode.

Study this mode and then practice playing it. Then play the licks that follow.

TRACK 261

G Phrygian Mode
(Minor Mode)

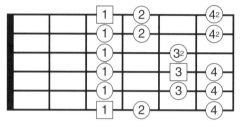

Licks Created from the G Phrygian Mode:

TRACKS 262–268

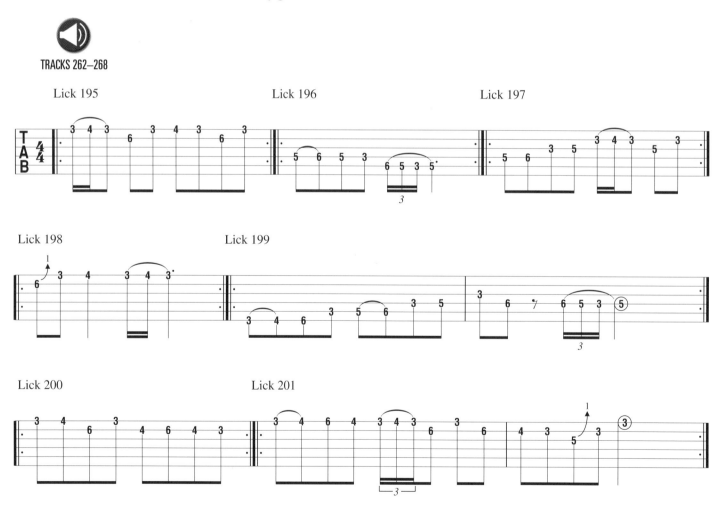

SAMPLE SOLO 12

This solo demonstrates the use of the G Phrygian mode and is played over Backing Track 10.

THE IONIAN MODE

The Ionian mode (also called the "major scale") is built from the "Do-Re-Mi-Fa-Sol-La-Ti-Do" notes that you probably sang as a child in school. It is form-equivalent to the Aeolian mode that you studied on page 54. Although all of the major modes possess a happy sound quality, the Ionian mode has one that is more mellow or pretty.

Shown below is the B♭ Ionian mode. Try to discern the B♭ major pentatonic scale residing in the mode, because it should make the mode easier to learn and use. The note with the arrow pointing to it is often played with the third finger when being bent (the same finger used for bending the note in the B♭ major pentatonic scale).

Study this mode and then practice playing it. Then play the licks that follow.

TRACK 270

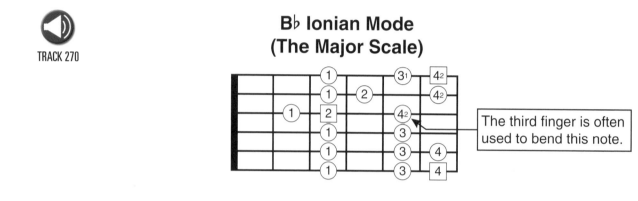

**B♭ Ionian Mode
(The Major Scale)**

The third finger is often used to bend this note.

Licks Created from the B♭ Ionian Mode:

TRACKS 271–278

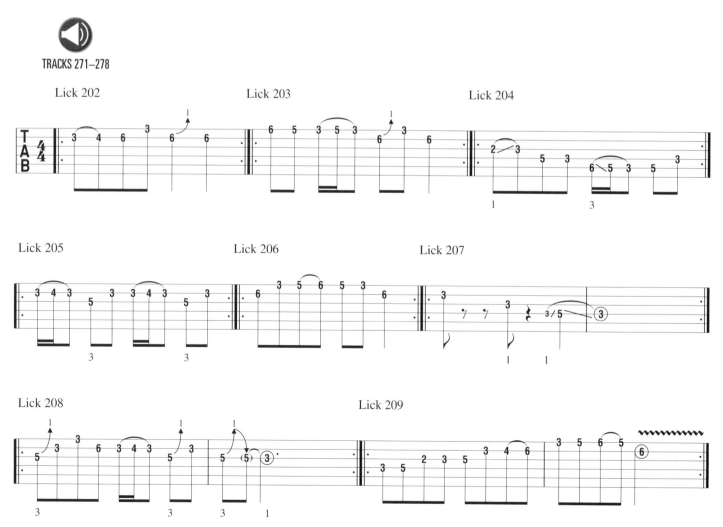

SAMPLE SOLO 13

This solo demonstrates the use of the G Ionian mode and is played over Backing Track 7. As previously noted, this track is in cut time and has a two-measure (four-beat) starting click.

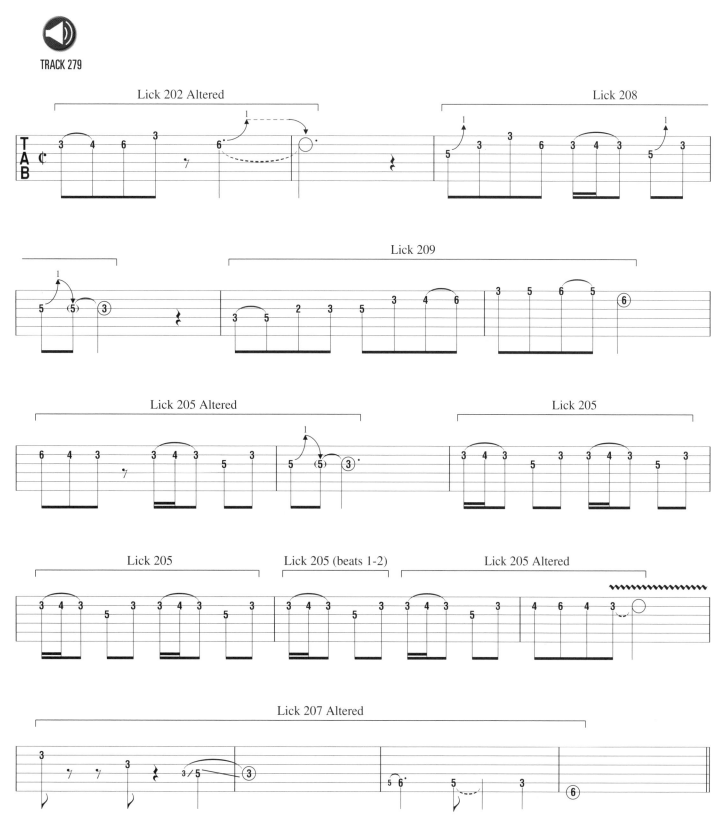

TRACK 279

SCALE
THE MIXOLYDIAN MODE

The Mixolydian mode is used occasionally by blues-based guitarists for soloing. Although it possesses a happy sound quality, the color is a bit more rugged—not quite as mellow or pretty as the Ionian mode. The Mixolydian mode is used in the melodies of such songs as the Champs' "Tequila" and the verses in the Beatles' "Norwegian Wood." It is form-equivalent to the Phrygian mode on page 57 and thus is an easy mode to master because of its smaller fingerboard span.

Shown below is the B♭ Mixolydian mode. As before, try to discern the B♭ major pentatonic scale residing in the mode.

Study this mode and then practice playing it. Then play the licks that follow.

TRACK 280

B♭ Mixolydian Mode
(Major Mode)

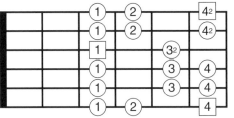

Licks Created from the B♭ Mixolydian Mode:

TRACKS 281–288

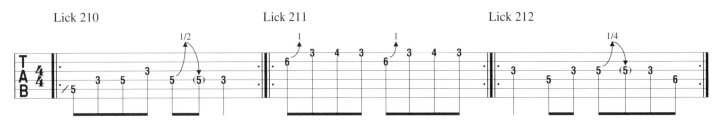

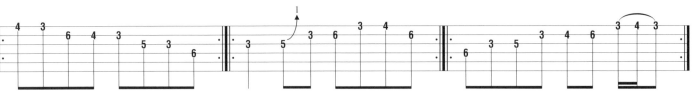

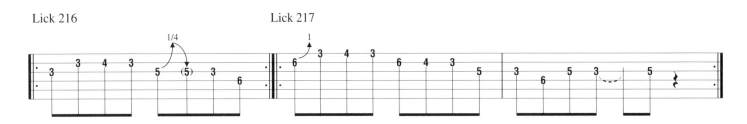

SAMPLE SOLO 14

This solo demonstrates the use of the G Mixolydian mode and is played over Backing Track 9.

TRACK 289

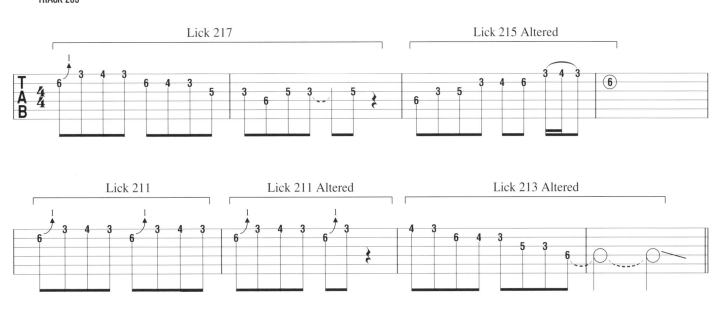

SCALE
THE LYDIAN MODE

Sometimes you may want to play a little bit off-center or what musicians call "outside." You can do this by choosing a mode that has notes which clash, to a certain degree, against the chords being played over. Although rarely used, the Lydian mode can be substituted for the Ionian mode to achieve this purpose.

The distinctive guitar riff of "Dancing Days" by Led Zeppelin was constructed from the Lydian mode. The mode is usually played over a major tonic chord, as was done in that song, or a sustained drone (tonic chords were explained on page 45). Experiment with it over other chords, as well, because you may come up with some unexpectedly pleasing results.

Shown below is the B♭ Lydian mode. It is form-equivalent to the Dorian mode on page 55. As before, try to discern the B♭ major pentatonic scale residing in the mode. The note with the arrow pointing to it is often played with the third finger when being bent (the same finger used when bending the note in the B♭ major pentatonic scale).

Study this mode and then practice playing it. Then play the licks that follow.

TRACK 290

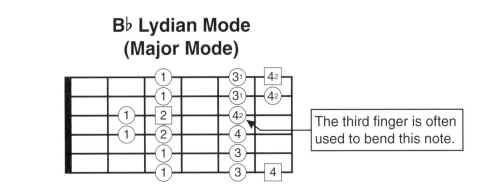

**B♭ Lydian Mode
(Major Mode)**

The third finger is often used to bend this note.

Licks Created From the B♭ Lydian Mode:

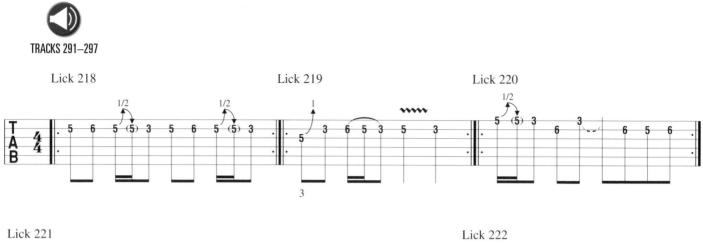

TRACKS 291–297

Lick 218   Lick 219   Lick 220

Lick 221   Lick 222

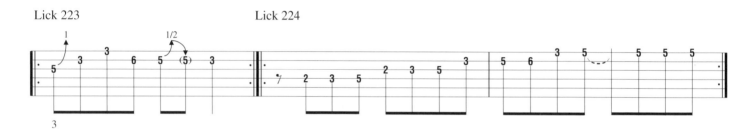

Lick 223   Lick 224

SAMPLE SOLO 15

This solo demonstrates the use of the G Lydian mode and is played over Backing Track 11.

TRACK 298

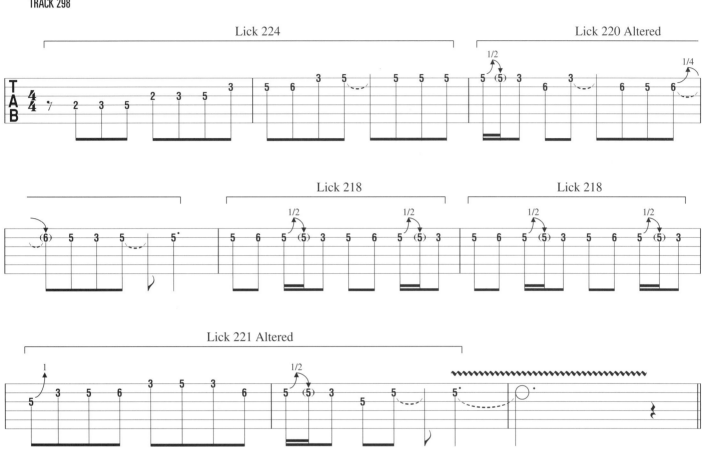

SCALE
THE PHRYGIAN DOMINANT SCALE

The Phrygian dominant scale is actually the Phrygian mode altered from a minor to major quality. This scale is very ethnic sounding (what many describe as "Spanish" or "Middle Eastern") and is typically used over a drone or chord progression involving two major chords a half step apart. Backing Track 11 is a drone and Backing Track 12 uses two major chords a half step apart, so you can solo with this scale over these two tracks. This was a favorite scale of surf music guitarist Dick Dale in the '60s.

On the following page is the G Phrygian dominant scale (this scale is also form-equivalent to the C harmonic minor scale). There are not any pentatonic scale formations residing in it, so it may be more difficult to learn. Also, when comparing it to the other modes and scales that you've learned, its note configuration is much more challenging to play.

Practice playing the scale. Then play the licks that follow.

TRACK 299

G Phrygian Dominant Scale

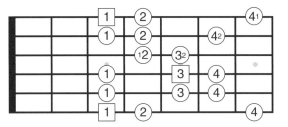

Licks Created from the G Phrygian Dominant Scale:

TRACKS 300–306

Lick 225   Lick 226   Lick 227

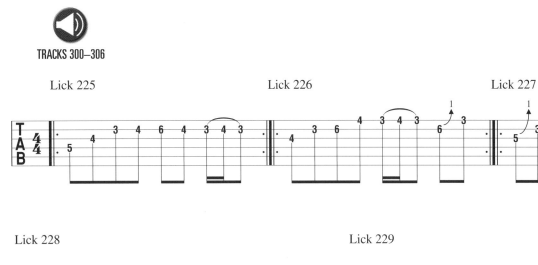

Lick 228   Lick 229

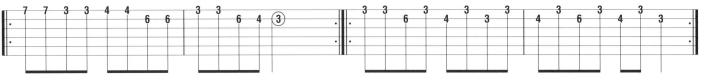

Lick 230   Lick 231

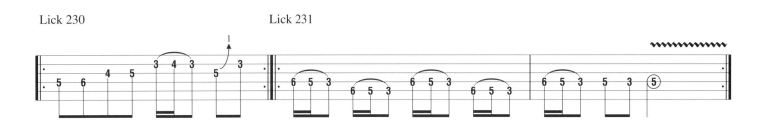

SAMPLE SOLO 16

This solo demonstrates the use of the G Phrygian dominant scale and is played over Backing Track 12.

TRACK 307

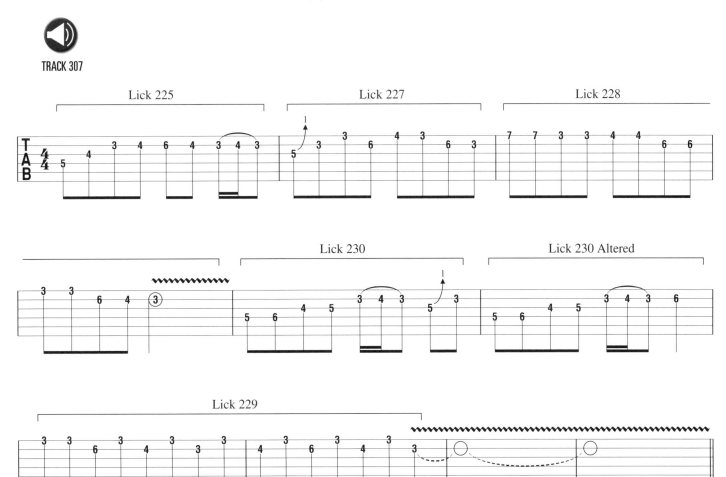

PART III

In Part III, we will be looking at alternate forms of each scale studied in Parts I and II. Learning these alternate forms will enable you to create solos that span the entire fingerboard and thus afford you a larger range of notes and other options to more fully express yourself. They are invaluable for the guitarist who wants more control and freedom over his or her instrument when soloing!

THE FIVE SCALE FORMS

In Parts I and II, you learned one form of each of the most popular scales used by guitarists for soloing (the extended versions of the scales are excluded here because they are actually a combination of three different forms, all of which are included in this section). Here, in Part III, you will be learning four more forms of each scale, which will make a total of five forms per scale that you can use for soloing.

To better understand what is meant by *scale forms*, think of it this way: each scale is comprised of a certain group of notes, so every form of a particular scale will also be composed of that group of notes. For example, although they have different configurations and locations on the fingerboard, the five forms of the G minor pentatonic scale on page 70 are all composed of the same group of notes: G, Bb, C, D, and F.

Using all five forms of a scale has many advantages. For one, you will have a larger range of notes at your disposal because the five forms collectively encompass the entire fingerboard. Secondly, redundancy in your solos will be reduced because your fingers will be forced to play the same group of notes in different configurations. Thirdly, two adjacent notes on two different strings in one form may be moved to just one string in another form, which will enable you to incorporate techniques that use two notes on one string, such as the hammer-on or pull-off.

MORE ABOUT THE FIVE SCALE FORMS

Shown on pages 70–80 are the five forms of each scale. They are placed in sequence from the lowest position on the fingerboard to the highest. The first form of each scale will always be one that you learned earlier in the book. After the fifth form, the sequence begins all over again on the fretboard, starting with the first form (an octave higher) and continuing up the fingerboard until running out of frets.

When shifting the forms up the fingerboard to play in other keys, the higher forms can be moved to the lower frets in front of the first form. For example, if the five forms of the G minor pentatonic scale on page 70 are moved up two frets to the key of A, then there is enough room for Form 5 to be placed on the lower frets before Form 1. Or, if moving to the key of B, both Form 4 and Form 5 can be placed before Form 1. (When shifting the forms down the fingerboard, the process is reversed.)

Read the following information concerning the scale forms on pages 70–80:

1. The gray circles on the diagrams correspond to the position markers on your guitar and are used as reference points to expedite the location of any particular fret. (Position markers are usually circles, but they may also be other shapes.)

2. The fingerings for these forms are shown only as a guide. You know from previous pages that the fingerings were sometimes altered to make some licks easier to play, so feel free to change the fingerings, if so desired.

3. You know that the circles with small numbers in them indicate notes that are typically bent by guitarists. However, you can actually bend any note so long as it's being bent to another note in the scale, so feel free to experiment bending other notes, too.

4. There are two ways to go about using the five forms to create a solo: one way is to pick a single form and solo with it exclusively, just like you've been doing up to this point. The other way is to solo by moving from one form to another. For example, you could create a lick using Form 1 and follow it with a lick created from Form 3, and so on. Or you could create half of a lick using one form and the other half using another form—the possibilities are endless (you will see licks created from the different forms in the sample solos in Part IV). Obviously, creating licks with the different forms is more difficult and requires good knowledge of the fingerings and location of each form being used, but it will yield results not possible from using one form alone.

MEMORIZING THE FIVE SCALE FORMS

MEMORIZING THE SCALE FORMS

Memorizing the five forms of the major and minor pentatonic and blues scales is easier than you might think. As you previously learned, the G minor pentatonic scale is form-equivalent to the B♭ major pentatonic scale. In other words, both of these scales have the same configuration and notes but their tonics are in different locations.

So, once you learn all five of the G minor pentatonic scale forms on page 70, you will have learned all five of the B♭ major pentatonic scale forms on page 71! Similarly, if you learn all five forms of the G blues scale on page 72, you will have learned all five forms of the B♭ major pentatonic scale with ♭3rd on page 73, because each scale on page 72 is form-equivalent to the scales on page 73!

Just remember that, when using form-equivalent scales, you must keep track of where the tonics are located. Also, the notes that are typically bent in two form-equivalent scales may be slightly different, so be aware of those differences, too.

MEMORIZING THE MODE FORMS

Memorizing the modes is almost as easy as the previous scales because the five forms of each of the six modes (the Phrygian dominant scale is excluded here) all have form-equivalents to one another.

For example, Form 1 of the G Aeolian mode is form-equivalent to Form 4 of the G Dorian mode; Form 2 of the G Aeolian mode is form-equivalent to Form 5 of the G Dorian mode; Form 3 of the G Aeolian mode is form-equivalent to Form 1 of the G Dorian mode; Form 4 of the G Aeolian mode is form-equivalent to Form 2 of the G Dorian mode; and Form 5 of the G Aeolian mode is form-equivalent to Form 3 of the G Dorian mode.

Additionally, Form 1 of the G Aeolian mode is form-equivalent to Form 3 of the G Phrygian mode, Form 2 of the G Aeolian mode is form-equivalent to Form 4 of the G Phrygian mode, and so on.

Form-equivalents are found throughout all of the modes. If you look closely at each mode and compare one to another, you will see that each form of one mode has a form equivalent to another. Consequently, this makes memorizing the modes easier because once you learn all five forms of one mode, you will know every form of *all* of the modes! Again, like the pentatonic and blues scales, you must keep track of where the tonics are located in each form and the differences in the notes that are typically bent.

Now study, memorize, and practice playing the five forms of each scale on the following pages.

G Minor Pentatonic Scale

Form 1

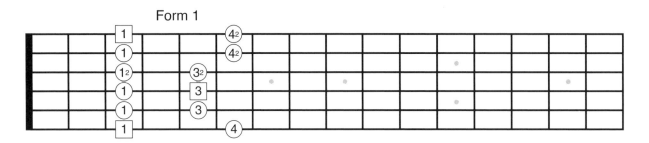

Form 2

Form 3

Form 4

Form 5

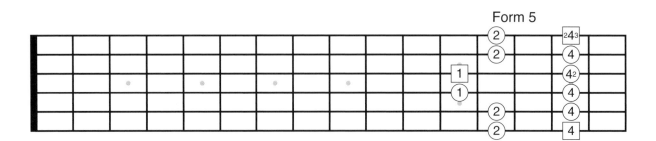

B♭ Major Pentatonic Scale

Form 1

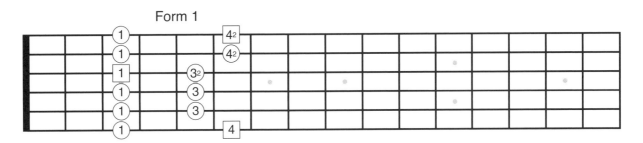

Form 2

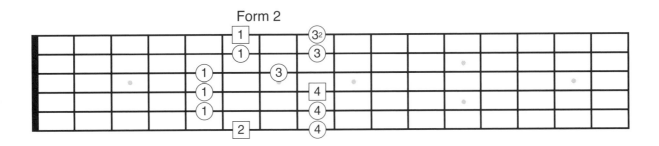

Form 3

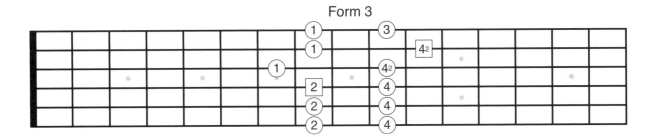

Form 4

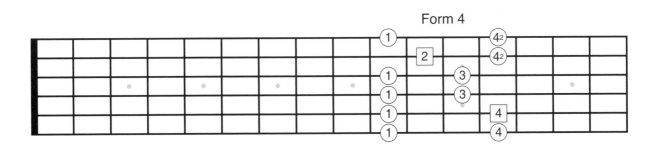

Form 5

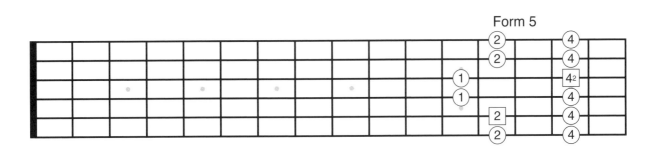

G Blues Scale

Form 1

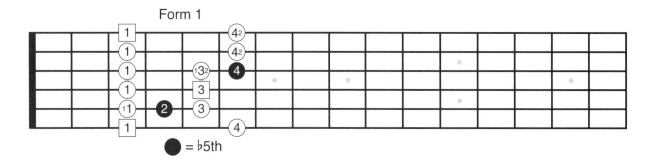

● = ♭5th

Form 2

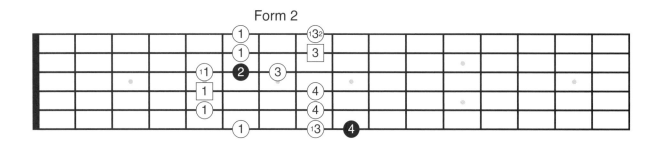

Form 3

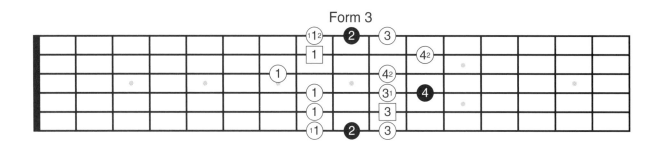

Form 4

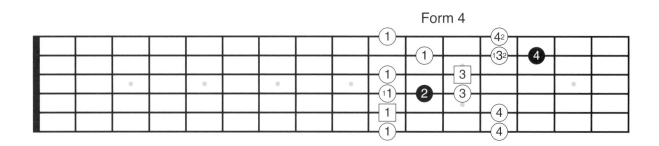

Form 5

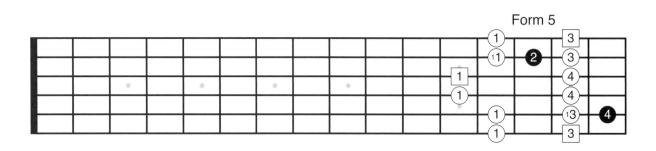

B♭ Major Pentatonic Scale with ♭3rd

Form 1

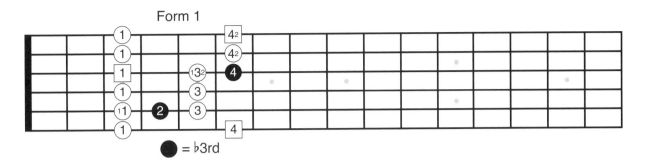

● = ♭3rd

Form 2

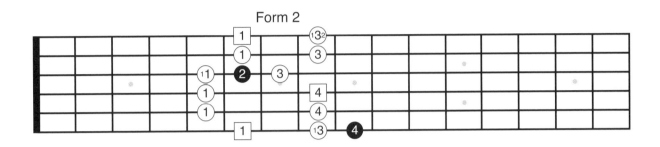

Form 3

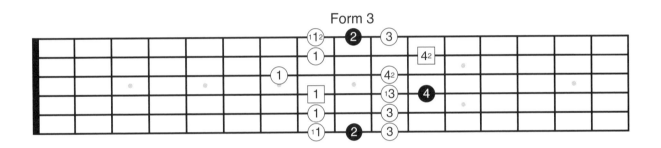

Form 4

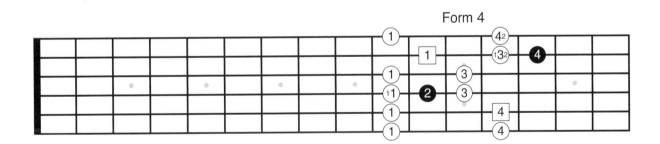

Form 5

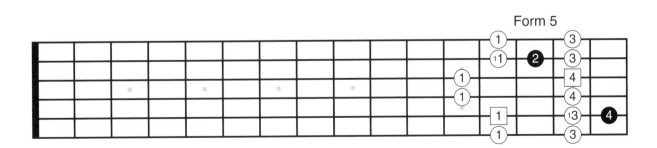

G Aeolian Mode

Form 1

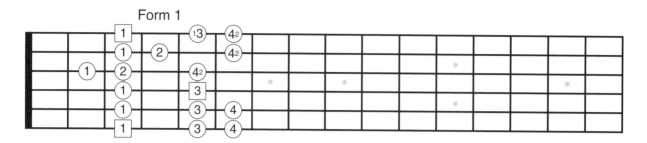

Form 2

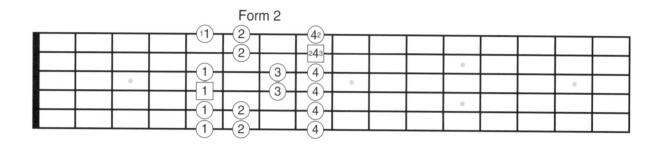

Form 3

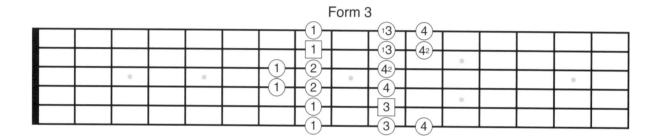

Form 4

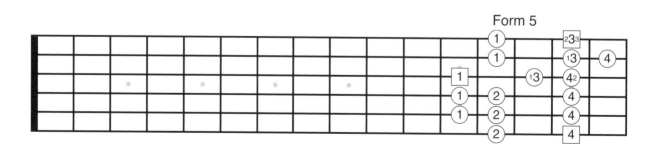

Form 5

G Dorian Mode

Form 1

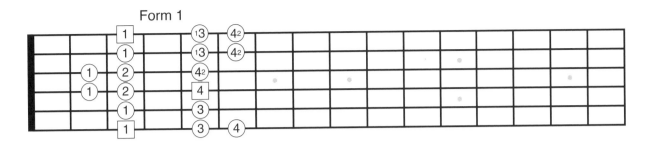

Form 2

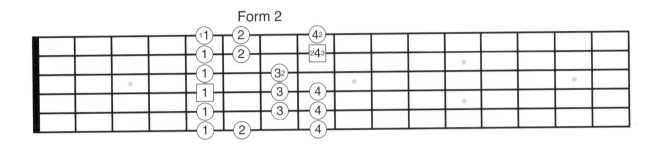

Form 3

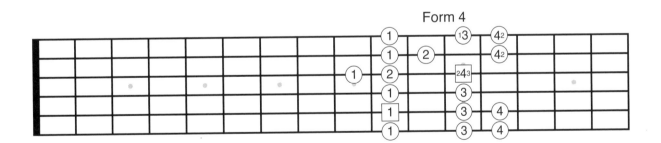

Form 4

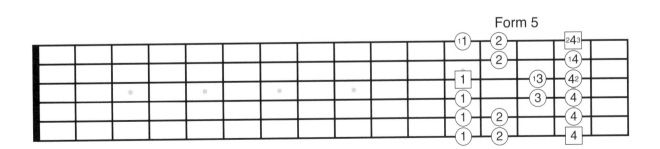

Form 5

G Phrygian Mode

Form 1

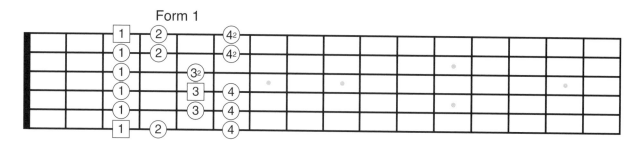

Form 2

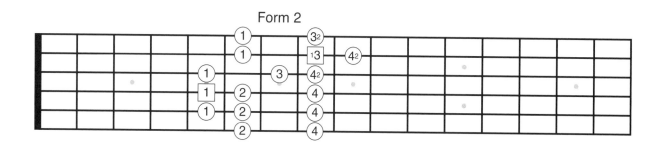

Form 3

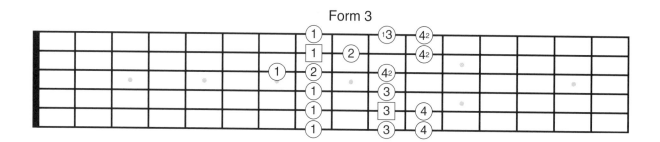

Form 4

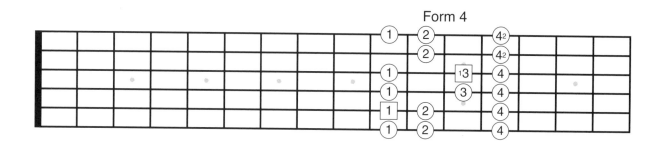

Form 5

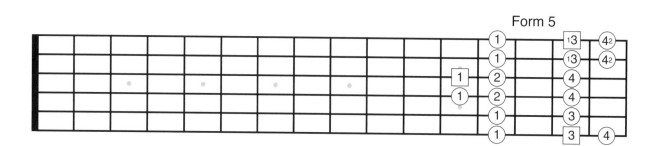

B♭ Ionian Mode

Form 1

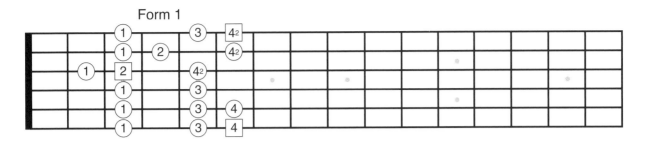

Form 2

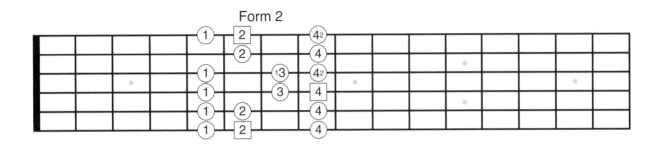

Form 3

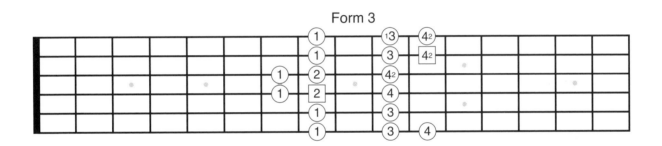

Form 4

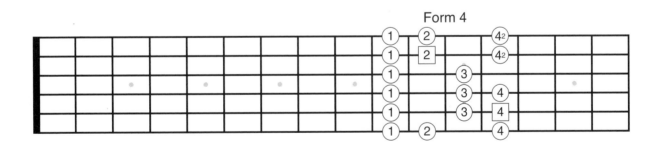

Form 5

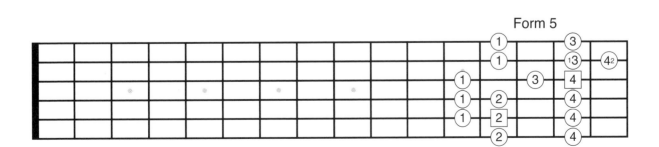

B♭ Mixolydian Mode

Form 1

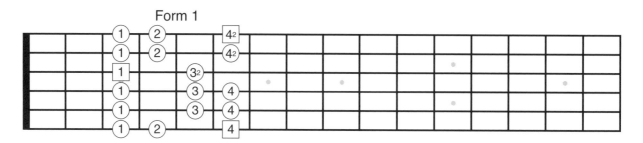

Form 2

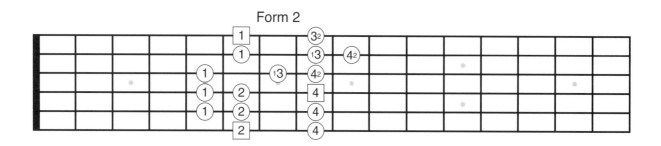

Form 3

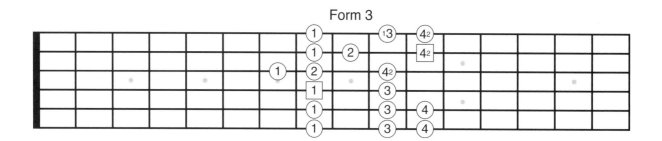

Form 4

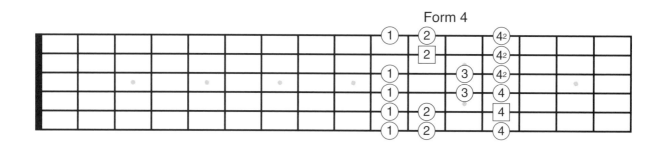

Form 5

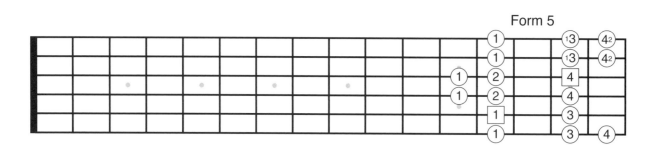

B♭ Lydian Mode

Form 1

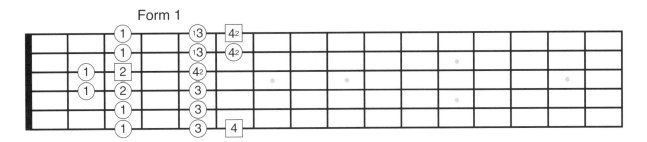

Form 2

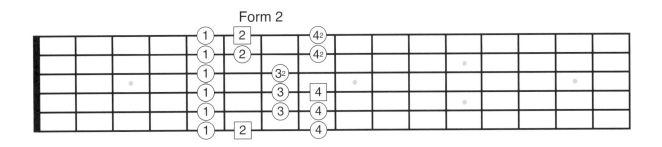

Form 3

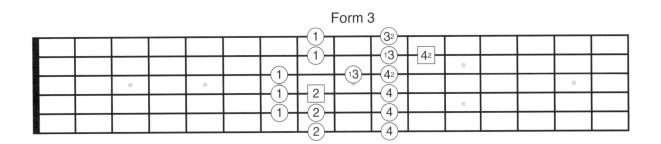

Form 4

Form 5

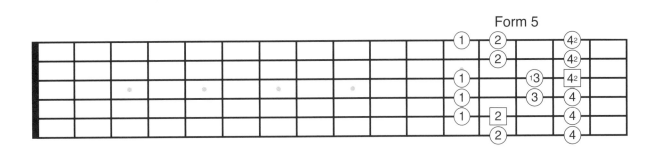

G Phrygian Dominant Scale

Form 1

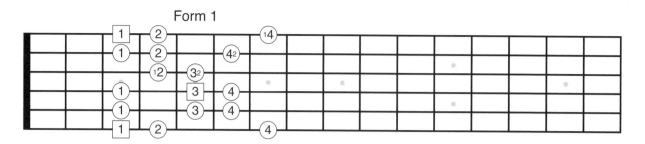

Form 2

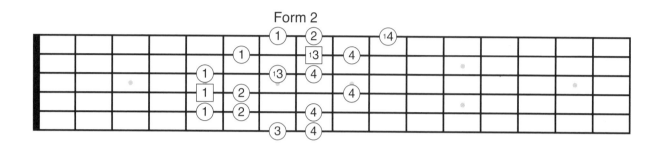

Form 3

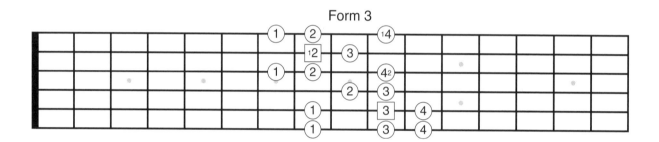

Form 4

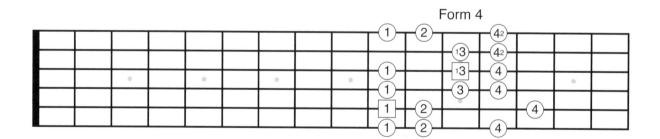

Form 5

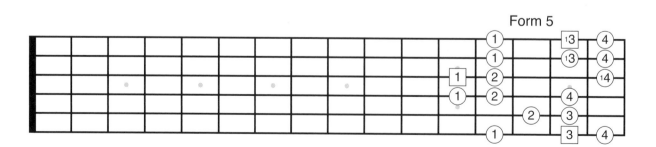

PART IV

In Part IV, you will be introduced to chordal soloing. This method of soloing involves using specific scales that are matched to the chords being soloed over—in other words, you will be changing scales with each new chord change to create your licks. We will also be investigating other ways to solo in the chordal fashion, such as employing 6ths and finger tapping arpeggios.

This section is a difficult one, but mastering its contents will enable you to create sounds that are not possible with modal soloing. So work hard on the material because you will come out a better soloist!

INTRODUCTION TO CHORDAL SOLOING

So far, you have been using the modal method to create your licks; that is, you chose one scale, moved it to the proper place on the fingerboard (as determined by the key), and used it over a group of chords without considering the names of the chords or any of their other attributes. Chordal soloing involves matching the scales to each chord being soloed over. This method of soloing takes more skill and concentration than does the modal method because you must think ahead to the next chord (letter name, major or minor quality, rhythmic position in the music, etc.) and the best way to solo over it. Although chordal soloing may seem hard at first, it will get easier as you study and practice it.

Use the four tips below to help integrate chordal soloing into your playing. It is also important when working through this section of the book that you analyze each solo to make sure you fully understand the method of chordal soloing being presented to you at the time.

FOUR TIPS WHEN USING CHORDAL SOLOING

1. Know All of the Notes on the Fingerboard
When using chordal soloing, you will be playing in different areas of the fingerboard and utilizing the different forms of the various scales you know, all of which will be constantly changing according to the chords being played. Knowing all of the notes on the fingerboard will help in locating everything more quickly and easily.

2. Know All Five Forms of Each Scale
When a chord changes, you will need to change from the scale you are using to one that matches the new chord. Finding the form that is closest to the one being used will make the transition between the two forms easier to execute. It will also help to make it easier to accomplish a smoother melodic connection between the two forms. Knowing all five forms of a scale makes it possible to use the form that is nearest to the one you are currently using.

3. Know Where Each Tonic Is Positioned in the Forms
Many times, you will want to solo in a particular area of the fingerboard, either because you are already in the specific area or you want to move to that area. Knowing the position of every tonic in the five forms of a scale makes it easier and quicker to find the form in a particular area of the fingerboard.

4. Put Some Time Between Your Licks
Putting some time between your licks means ending a lick a couple of beats or more before the next lick begins. Giving yourself some time between the licks is especially helpful at this point because chordal soloing is new to you. This extra time will allow you to think about how you're going to solo over the next chord and also make moving (if desired) to a new fingerboard location easier and less foreboding.

When analyzing the solos in this section, you will find that many times there is *not* any time placed between the licks, but just the opposite. As you become more advanced with the chordal method of soloing, putting time between your licks becomes less of a helpful and needed action, and more of an expressive, artistic one.

PENTATONIC SCALES WITH CHORDS

When using pentatonic scales with chords, choose the pentatonic scale that has the same letter name and major or minor quality as the chord being played over (the minor pentatonic scale is still interchangeable with the blues scale, and the major pentatonic scale is still interchangeable with the major pentatonic scale with ♭3rd). For example, use the D major pentatonic scale over a D major chord (D) and the C minor pentatonic scale over a C minor chord (Cm).

Shown below are two solos with licks created from pentatonic scales matched according to the chords being played over. Study the solos and then try playing them. The scale and form used to create each lick are shown above the tab.

SAMPLE SOLO 17

This solo is played over Backing Track 13.

TRACK 308

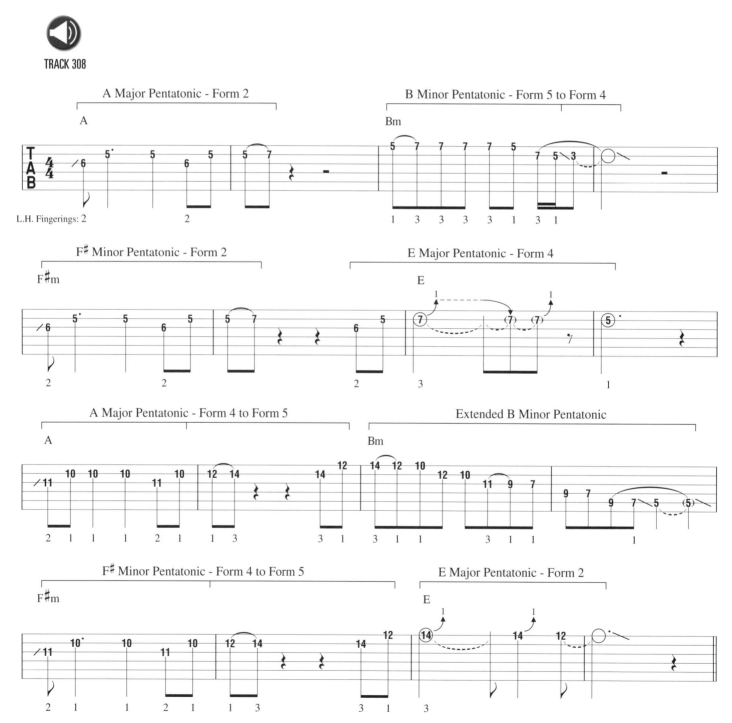

SAMPLE SOLO 18

This solo also matches pentatonic scales with their proper chords. It is a hard-driving blues with an eighth-note swing feel. The solo is played over Backing Track 14.

TRACK 309

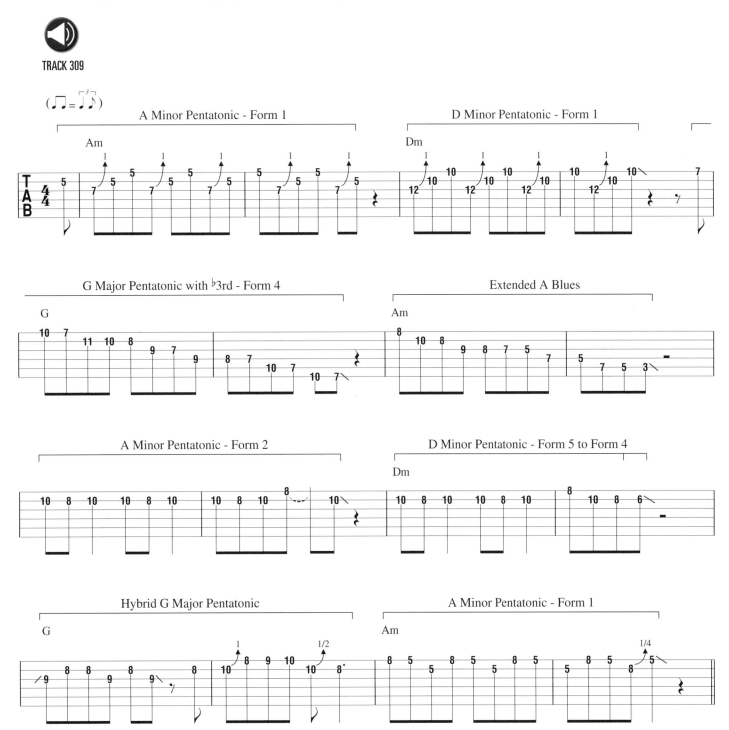

PHRYGIAN DOMINANT SCALE WITH CHORDS

The Phrygian dominant scale is typically used over the V ("five") chord from a minor key—a V chord being a major or dominant 7th chord with the same letter name as the 5th of the tonic chord. For example, the V chord in the key of C minor is G (or G7) because the 5th of a C minor chord is a G note. As shown on the next page, the scale can also be used over secondary V chords of minor chords in the key—a secondary V chord is a major or dominant 7th chord with the same letter name as the 5th of another chord in the key. Pentatonic scales were used to create the licks over the remaining chords in Sample Solos 19 and 20.

The above material may be difficult to understand, especially if you are not schooled in music theory, but listen closely to the unique sound of the Phrygian dominant licks played over the different V chords. Because the scale has such a singular sound, your ear may be reliable enough to discern where it can be used. You can also consult a music dictionary for a better understanding of the material by looking up the terms "dominent chords" and "secondary dominant chords."

SAMPLE SOLO 19

This solo is in the key of B minor. The F♯ major chord is the major V chord of B minor, so the Phrygian dominant scale is used to solo over it. The solo is played over Backing Track 15.

TRACK 310

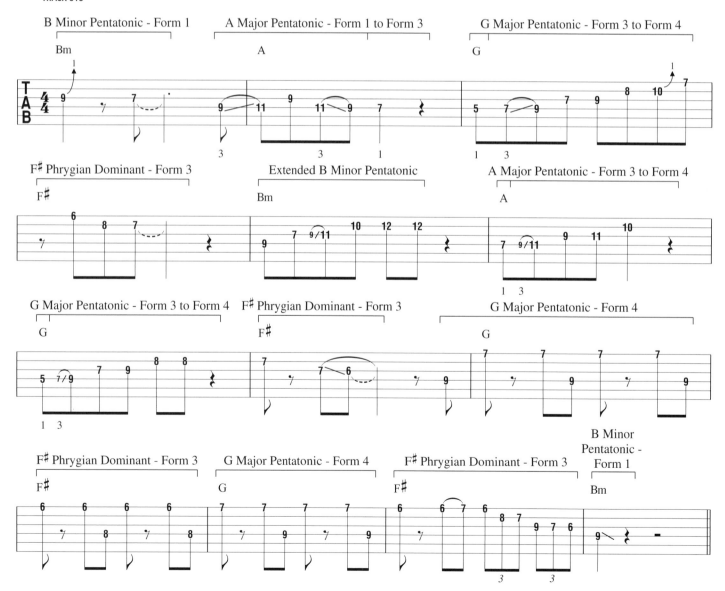

SAMPLE SOLO 20

This solo has more of a smooth jazz feel to it. It is in the key of C major and includes three secondary V chords: A7, E7, and D7. These chords are V chords of chords in the key of C major: A7 is the V chord of Dm, E7 is the V chord of Am, and D7 is the V chord of G major. Since the A7 and E7 are V chords of minor keys, the Phrygian dominant scale is used. Since the D7 is the V chord of a major key, the major pentatonic scale is used. This solo is played over Backing Track 16.

TRACK 311

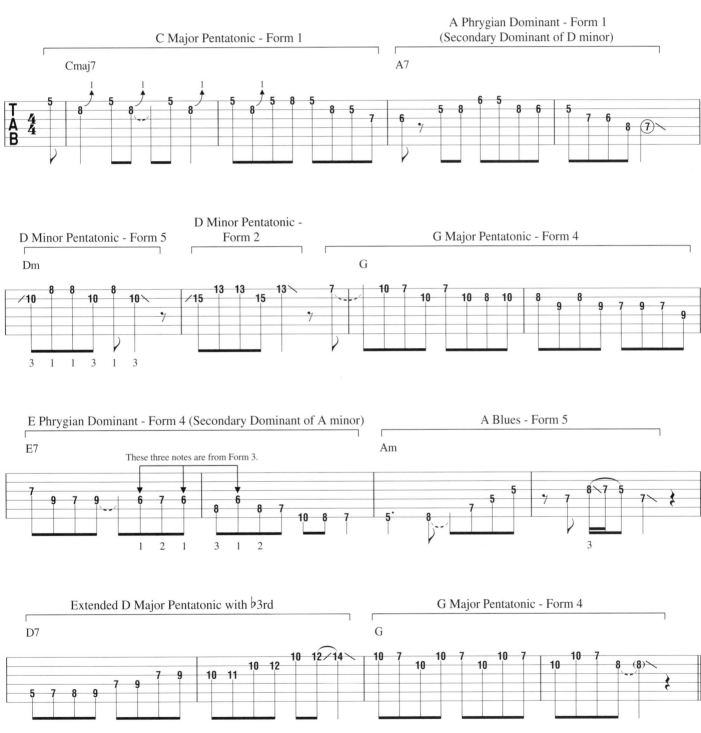

MINOR PENTATONIC SCALE WITH MAJOR 3RDS

When a minor pentatonic scale is used in a major key, soloists often add notes called *major 3rds*. Licks created with these notes can be employed using one of two methods: 1) they can be used over the tonic chord in the progression, or 2) they can be used over any major chord in the progression. When they are used over major chords other than the tonic, as in the second method, the name of the scale from which the licks are derived must match the major chords being played.

Shown below is the G minor pentatonic scale with the added major 3rds, indicated by black circles. Below the scale are licks created from the scale that use the major 3rds. Use these licks when playing over a G major chord. If you want to use them over other major chords, you must shift them up or down the fingerboard so that their letter name matches the chord you are playing over. For example, if you played Lick 232 over a C chord, you would start it on the tenth fret; if you played it over an A chord, you would start it on the seventh fret, etc.

Try playing the licks and then play and analyze the solo that follows.

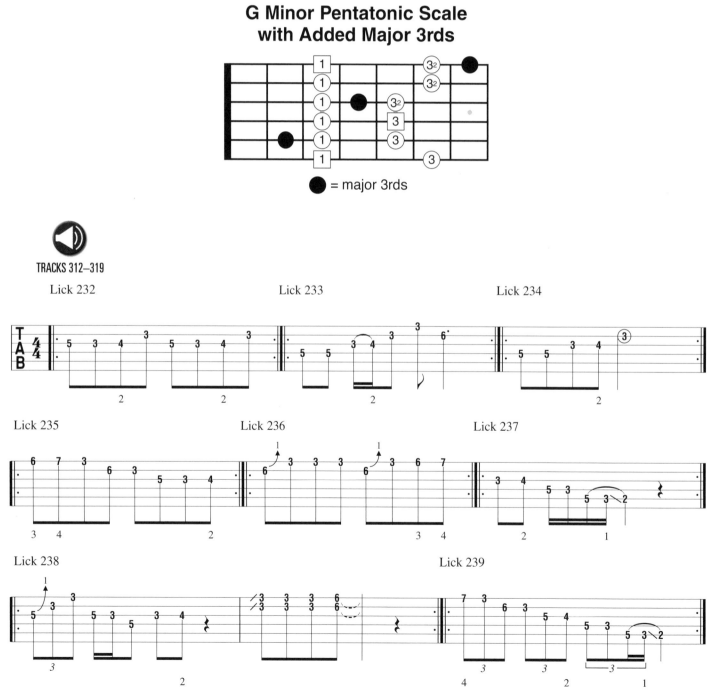

G Minor Pentatonic Scale with Added Major 3rds

● = major 3rds

TRACKS 312–319

Lick 232   Lick 233   Lick 234

Lick 235   Lick 236   Lick 237

Lick 238   Lick 239

SAMPLE SOLO 21

This solo is in the key of G major and played over Backing Track 2. It is a 12-bar blues played twice. In the first 12 measures (first three lines), the major 3rds (labeled "M3") are only used over the tonic chord, G. In the last 12 measures (last three lines), the licks shift up the fingerboard to match the chord being played. For example, the G lick in the first two measures of line 4 (measures 13–14) is shifted up five frets to make it a C lick (measures 17–18).

This solo has a straight eighth-note feel and incorporates many of the licks (altered and unaltered) from the previous page.

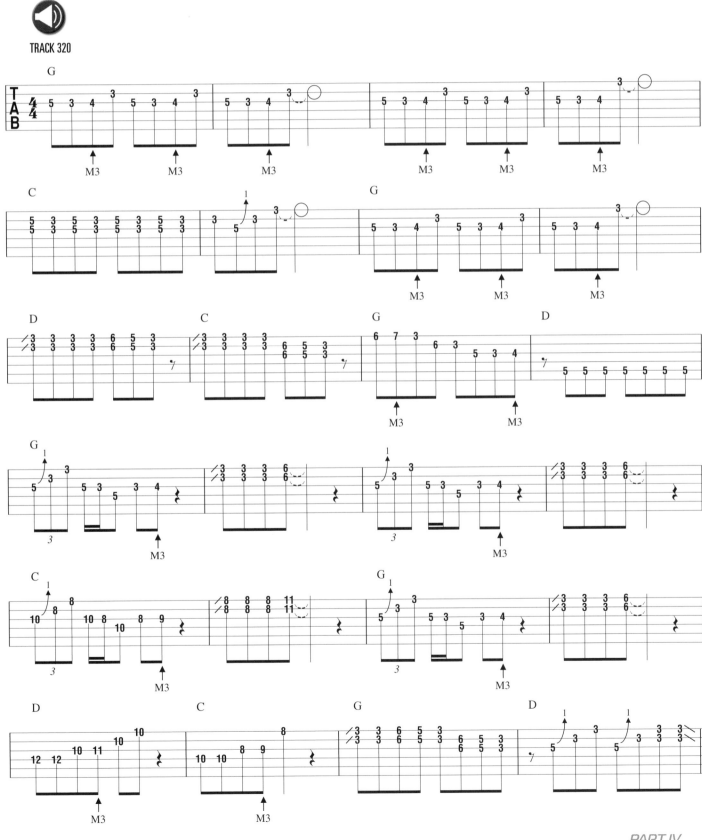

TRACK 320

SIXTHS

Blues-based guitarists sometimes use double stops called 6ths. The most commonly used 6ths have an unused string positioned in between the two fretted strings, as shown in the two examples below.

The 6ths shown in the first example are to be played over a G major chord and the ones shown in the second example over a G minor chord. Each pair of notes can be played either individually or together. When playing both notes together, you can either dispense with the pick and just use your right-hand thumb and index finger to pluck, or you can strike the third string with your pick and the first string with the middle finger of your right hand (playing with the pick and fingers in this fashion is called *hybrid picking*).

Try playing the two examples.

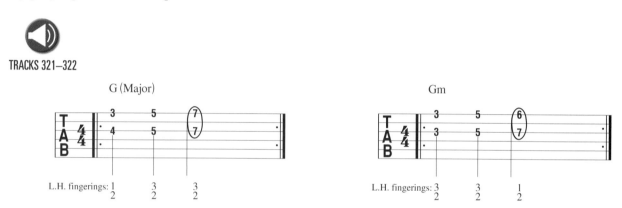

TRACKS 321–322

The licks shown below were created from the G major group shown in the first example above. Try playing them. Then convert the licks to the G minor group shown in the second example above. When using these 6ths in a solo, you must move them to match the chords that are being played. For example, your first finger would be on the eighth fret if you played Lick 240 over a C major chord; your third finger would be on the seventh fret if you played Lick 240 and converted it for a B minor chord, and so on.

TRACKS 323–329

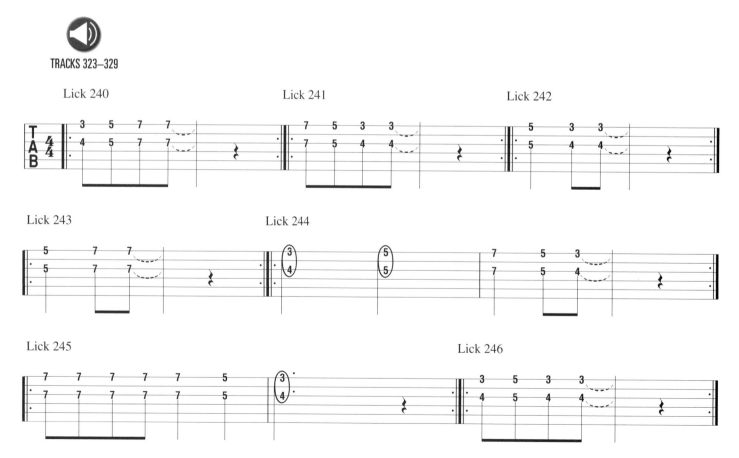

SAMPLE SOLO 22

This entire solo was composed exclusively with 6ths. It was created from altered versions of Licks 244 and 245 and played with the right-hand thumb and index finger. When analyzing the solo, disregard the numbers in the chord symbols because they do not affect the usage of the 6ths. The solo is played over Backing Track 16, the same backing track used for Sample Solo 20.

TRACK 330

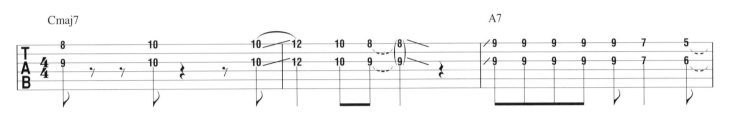

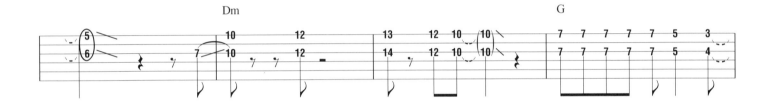

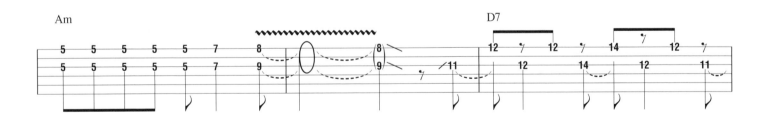

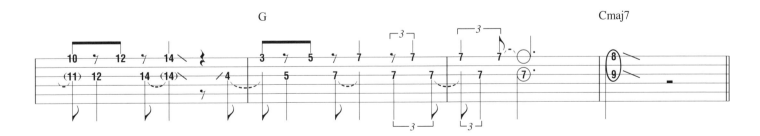

FINGER TAPPING

Shown in the example below is a somewhat newer technique brought to the forefront in the '70s by guitarist Eddie Van Halen. This technique is called *finger tapping* and involves a right-hand-finger hammer-on called a *tap*, which is indicated by an uppercase "T" over the note. There are many finger-tapping patterns, but the example below demonstrates one of the easier ones for beginners.

When playing the example, you must forcibly tap down (like a hammer-on) on the first note with the middle finger of the right hand (this assumes that you are holding a pick between your thumb and first finger). Some guitarists use their index finger to tap while temporarily holding the pick in the palm of their hand with the other fingers. The tapped note is immediately followed by a pull-off to the second note and then another pull-off to the third note. Listen to the example and then try playing it.

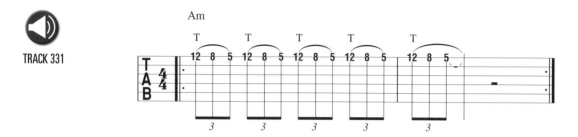

TRACK 331

Finger tapping, as studied here, will consist of playing the notes of a chord in succession. Playing the chord notes separately in this manner—one after another—is called an *arpeggio*. Below is a chart showing the notes used to construct major, minor, and diminished chords. For example, a B♭ chord is constructed from the notes B♭–D–F, an E minor chord is constructed from the notes E–G–B, and a B diminished chord is constructed from the notes B–D–F. The example above uses the notes from an A minor chord: A–C–E.

When using finger tapping to play a chord, first use the chord construction chart below to find the notes of a particular chord. Then use the fingerboard diagram on page 6 to locate the notes on one of the guitar strings. The notes can be mixed up in any order, but the first note should always be the tapped note.

Go to Sample Solo 23 and see how it is constructed from only the notes of the chords being played over.

CHORD CONSTRUCTION CHART

CHORD	MAJOR	MINOR	DIMINISHED
A	A – C♯ – E	A – C – E	A – C – E♭
B♭ (A♯)	B♭ – D – F	B♭ – D♭ – F	B♭ – D♭ – F♭
B	B – D♯ – F♯	B – D – F♯	B – D – F
C	C – E – G	C – E♭ – G	C – E♭ – G♭
D♭ (C♯)	D♭ – F – A♭	D♭ – F♭ – A♭	D♭ – F♭ – A♭♭
D	D – F♯ – A	D – F – A	D – F – A♭
E♭ (D♯)	E♭ – G – B♭	E♭ – G♭ – B♭	E♭ – G♭ – B♭♭
E	E – G♯ – B	E – G – B	E – G – B♭
F	F – A – C	F – A♭ – C	F – A♭ – C♭
F♯ (G♭)	F♯ – A♯ – C♯	F♯ – A – C♯	F♯ – A – C
G	G – B – D	G – B♭ – D	G – B♭ – D♭
A♭ (G♯)	A♭ – C – E♭	A♭ – C♭ – E♭	A♭ – C♭ – E♭♭

SAMPLE SOLO 23

This solo demonstrates the finger-tapping pattern from the previous example and is composed entirely of arpeggios. Analyze the solo by looking at the notes used in each chord and comparing them to the chord construction chart. You will see that the notes used for a chord consist only of the notes belonging to that particular chord. The hard-driving backing and diminished chords (chords with a circle as their symbol) used for this solo are stylistically typical of the finger-tapping technique. The solo is played over Backing Track 17.

TRACK 332

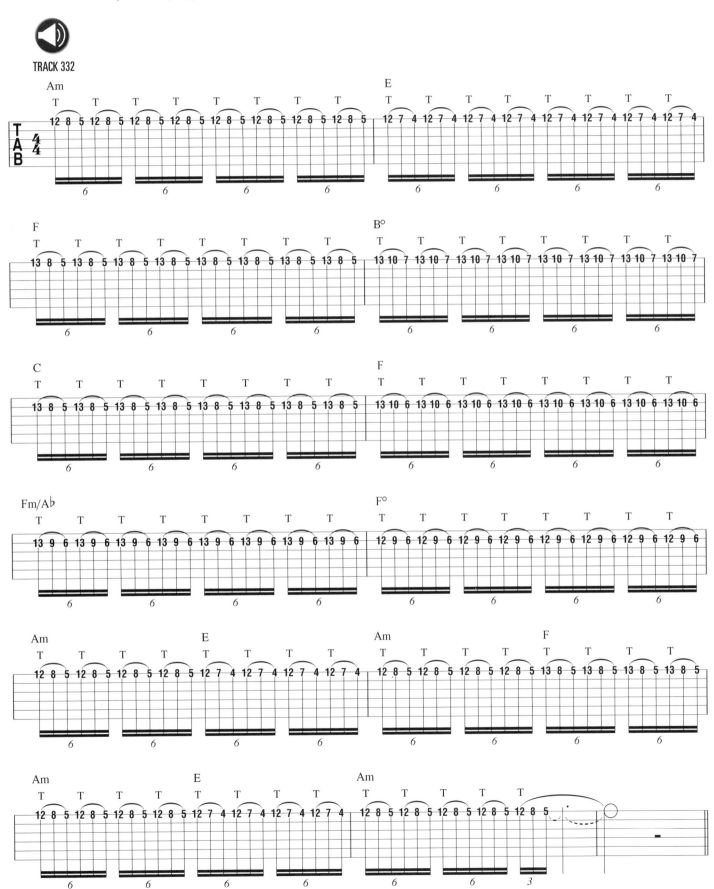

APPENDIX – THE BACKING TRACKS

Shown below and on the following pages is a listing of the backing tracks used for the sample solos in the book, and which you can use to create your own solos. Backing Tracks 1–12 were used for the sample solos in Parts I and II and work well for modal soloing. Backing Tracks 13–17 were used for the sample solos in Part IV and work well for chordal soloing. (Backing Track 2 was used for the modal soloing in Sample Solo 2 and Sample Solo 10, as well as for the chordal soloing in Sample Solo 21.)

The listings for Backing Tracks 1–12 show the chord progressions being used for each track, the key of each track, and the appropriate scales that can be used for soloing over each track. Practice making your own modal solos by creating new licks from the scales and playing them over these tracks. You should also play any licks that you learn in Parts I and II over these tracks to hear how they sound in a musical context.

The listing of Backing Tracks 13–17 start on page 94. Use these tracks to practice chordal soloing. Because these tracks are meant to be used for chordal soloing, only their chord progressions are shown.

You may notice that the blues scale and the major pentatonic scale with ♭3rd are not included in the listings. The reason for this is to avoid redundancy because, as stated previously in the book, you can always use the blues scale interchangeably with the minor pentatonic scale, and the major pentatonic scale with ♭3rd interchangeably with the major pentatonic scale.

BACKING TRACK 1: Key of G minor. Use the minor pentatonic scale or the Dorian mode.

BACKING TRACK 2: Key of G major. Use the minor or major pentatonic scale or the Dorian mode. This track is a blues with a straight-eighths feel.

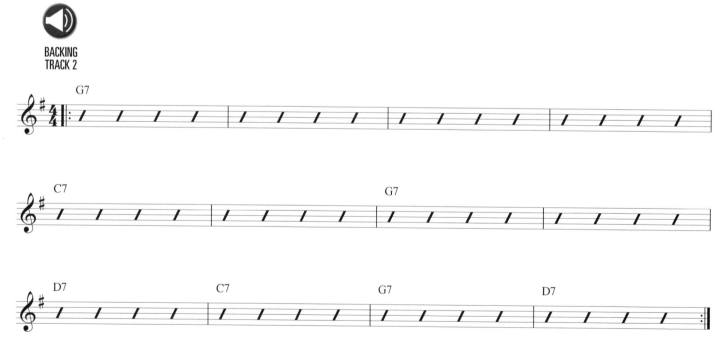

BACKING TRACK 3: Key of B minor. Use the minor pentatonic scale. This track has a swung-eighths feel.

BACKING TRACK 4: Key of C major. Use the minor or major pentatonic scale or the Dorian mode. This track is a blues with a swung-eighths feel.

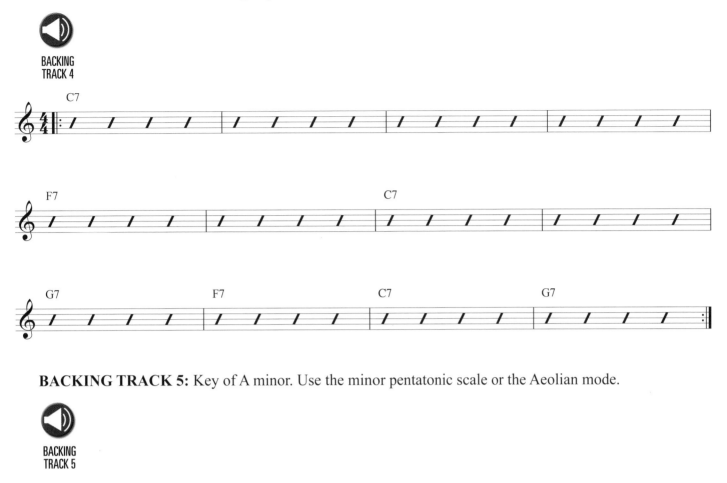

BACKING TRACK 5: Key of A minor. Use the minor pentatonic scale or the Aeolian mode.

BACKING TRACK 6: Key of Bb major. Use the major or minor pentatonic scale or the Dorian mode. This track has a swung-eighths feel.

BACKING TRACK 7: Key of Bb major. Use the Ionian mode or the major pentatonic scale. This track is in cut time and has a two-measure (four-beat) starting click.

BACKING TRACK 8: Key of G minor. Use the Aeolian mode or the minor pentatonic scale.

BACKING TRACK 9: Key of B♭ major. Use the Mixolydian mode or the major pentatonic scale.

BACKING
TRACK 9

BACKING TRACK 10: Key of G minor. Use the Phrygian mode or the minor pentatonic scale.

BACKING
TRACK 10

BACKING TRACK 11: B♭ drone (key of B♭). Use the Lydian mode or the Phrygian dominant scale. The discordant notes in either scale sound especially good when emphasized against this track.

BACKING
TRACK 11

BACKING TRACK 12: Key of G major. Use the Phrygian dominant scale.

BACKING
TRACK 12

Listed below and on the following page are Backing Tracks 13–17. With the exception of Sample Solo 21, they were used for Sample Solos 17–23 in Part IV. Backing Track 2 was used for Sample Solo 21, so it is not listed here (since it was already listed on page 92). These backing tracks work well for practicing chordal soloing.

BACKING TRACK 13: This backing track was used for Sample Solo 17.

BACKING
TRACK 13

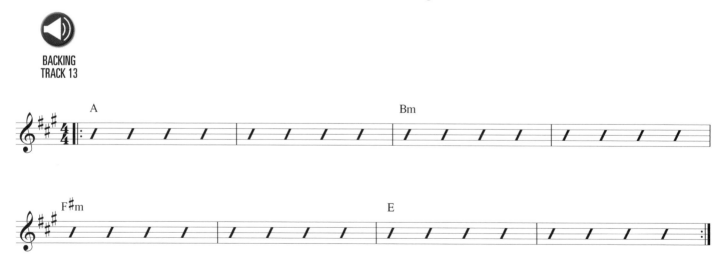

BACKING TRACK 14: This backing track was used for Sample Solo 18.

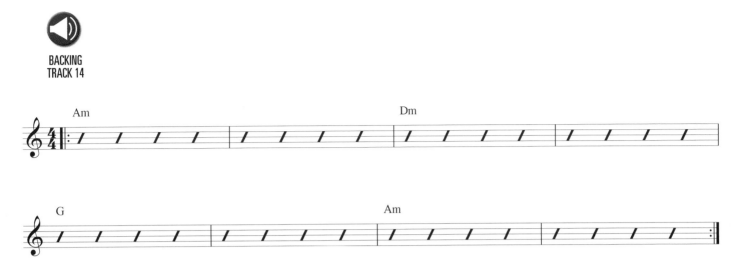

BACKING TRACK 15: This backing track was used for Sample Solo 19.

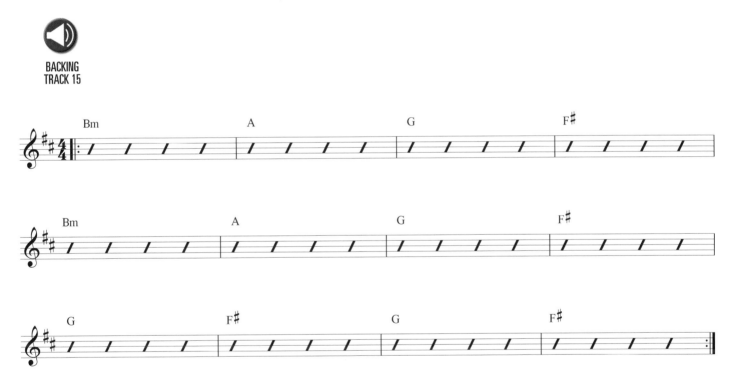

BACKING TRACK 16: This backing track was used for both Sample Solo 20 and Sample Solo 22.

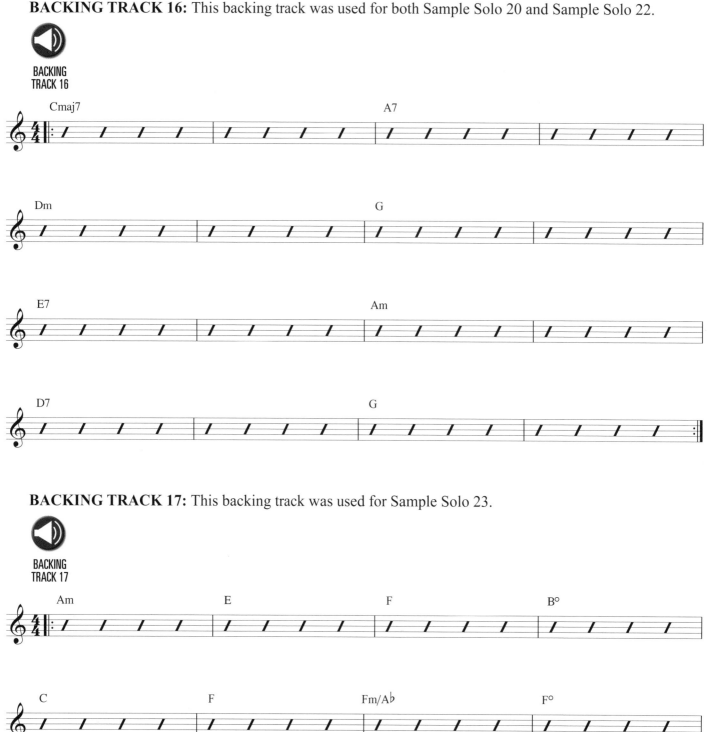

BACKING TRACK 17: This backing track was used for Sample Solo 23.

ABOUT THE AUTHOR

Jeff Clementi has been successfully teaching guitar since 1976 and averages 80 private lessons with his students per week. In addition to teaching, Jeff has performed throughout the Midwest, playing a variety of musical styles, both as a soloist and as part of an ensemble, which sometimes includes opening for major artists. He also enjoys writing music ranging from pop songs to orchestral compositions. Jeff resides in southeastern Wisconsin and holds a Bachelor's degree in Fine Arts from UW-Parkside.